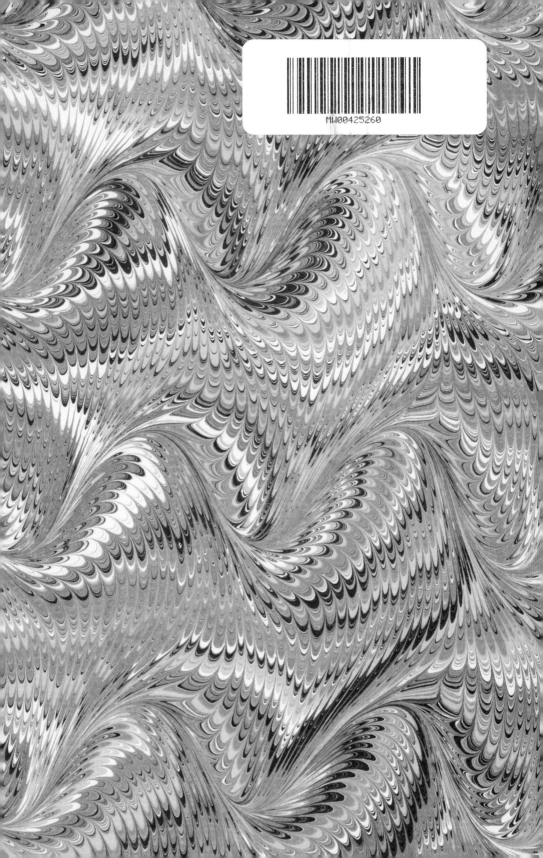

THE
WITCH'S DOOR

THE
WITCH'S DOOR

ODDITIES & TALES
from the ESOTERIC *to the* EXTREME

Ryan Matthew Cohn
& Regina M. Rossi

WITH JIM RULAND

CHRONICLE PRISM

Library of Congress Cataloging-in-Publication Data available.

ISBN 978-1-7972-2958-4

Manufactured in China.

Design by Pamela Geismar.
Typeset in Adobe Caslon Pro, Antique Macabre Ornaments,
Charcuterie Ornaments, Engravers Roman, and FCaslon Twelve.

10 9 8 7 6 5 4 3 2 1

Chronicle books and gifts are available at special quantity
discounts to corporations, professional associations, literacy
programs, and other organizations. For details and discount
information, please contact our premiums department at
corporatesales@chroniclebooks.com or at 1-800-759-0190.

 CHRONICLE PRISM

Chronicle Prism is an imprint of Chronicle Books LLC,
680 Second Street, San Francisco, California 94107

www.chronicleprism.com

TO ALL THE BLACK SHEEP
WHO HAVE ALWAYS FELT OUT OF STEP

CONTENTS

X. THE RICHARD HARRIS COLLECTION

EPILOGUE: BEYOND THE WITCH'S DOOR

WARNING

You are about to enter a realm of the strange and unusual. The death-positive compendium of oddities and curiosities you hold in your hands represents our lifelong fascination with the macabre and the bizarre. While some will find these artifacts to be an affront to good manners and common decency, we see great beauty in the journey our bodies take long after life deserts us. Some of the artifacts you will encounter in these pages stretch the limits of credulity; others are simply shocking. We present them to you with the assurance of our respect for the dead and our gratitude for all they have taught us.

Also, this book may, or may not, be haunted.

Enter at your own risk . . .

THE
WITCH'S
DOOR

OLD JEF

OLD JEF
Ryan & Regina

The first time we laid eyes on the Witch's Door, we knew it was something special.

We'd just acquired the collection of a friend whom we'll call Nick Parmesan. He was given the moniker because his parents ran a neighborhood deli in Brooklyn that made the best chicken parmesan known to humankind.

Nick was an odd guy. He was a former New York Police Department sergeant who took early leave from the force after 9/11. Some people travel when they retire. Others go to the beach. Nick caught the collecting bug. He did a lot of his collecting online, but he was also a fixture at many of the flea markets and antique shops where we did business. All collectors are secretive, but Nick took it to the extreme and had many enemies. Despite some ups and downs in our long relationship, we considered Nick a friend.

He was also a hoarder.

We'd only been to Nick's apartment in Brooklyn a handful of times. Although he was proud of his collection, he didn't like people poking around his stuff. Nick had an incredible eye, but his collection was a mess. It was so vast and disorganized that he didn't have a way to display it. We didn't realize how serious his hoarding problem had become until after he passed away.

There's no other way to put this: Nick's apartment was a horror show. Boxes and bags were piled up all over the place. The stacks rose from the floor and went all the way up to the ceiling. The place was dark and dangerous and in disrepair. Walking from one room to the next was an adventure because each step required moving piles of Nick's stuff out of the way.

These obstacles aside, Nick's collection was jaw-dropping. We couldn't believe the quality of the stuff he had in there. Suits of armor. A squad of skeletons. Exquisite eighteenth-century Italian figures. Amid the towers of garbage and junk, we found unusual sculptures, boxes of teeth, and antiquities rare enough to be displayed in a museum.

When we acquired Nick's collection, we agreed to clear out his apartment so that it would be ready for its new occupants to rent. As is usually the case in situations where someone passes away unexpectedly, we didn't have much time to prepare for the cleanup, and everything had to go. We rented some trucks and enlisted the aid of a full-scale crew, but toward the end of our first day we had to face the truth: We'd underestimated the amount of stuff that Nick had crammed inside his apartment. We'd barely made a dent in it, and we were completely overwhelmed.

As we were getting ready to leave for the day, something caught our attention. We couldn't tell what it was, but it looked like a piece of antique furniture. At first we thought it was a headboard, but it was far too big for that.

After shifting some boxes around, we noticed what looked like a rough wooden door with hand-forged wrought-iron hardware leaning against the wall. It was massive—that's what caught our attention—but there was too much stuff in front of it to get a good look. Now that our curiosity was piqued, we needed to know exactly what we were looking at.

We kept moving things around until we could see the piece properly. It was definitely a door, and it wasn't in very good condition. The wood was scratched and scarred. It was obviously very old. Although it was far from beautiful, there was something about the door that called to us.

It was getting late and becoming dark inside the apartment. Our bodies ached from moving Nick's belongings around all day. We were positive we'd never seen this object in his apartment or heard him talk about it before, which meant one of two things: Either he'd acquired it recently or he'd kept it hidden from us.

Why would he do that?

We didn't always understand Nick's impulses, but we trusted his taste. We knew it had to be *something*.

Once we brought the antique out into the light, we noticed something very unusual. In the upper part of the door someone had carved a figure into the wood. This wasn't a decorative detail. The carving was ugly and crude, but because it had faded with time it was also easy to miss in the gloom of Nick's apartment. The door had been defaced with the carving of an image of a sinister-looking woman.

Above the figure, the words OLD JEF had been inscribed, which was an Old English term for the devil.

This carving had been made as a warning to others.

Old Jef lives here.

A she-devil.

A witch.

We looked at each other in amazement.

What the hell had Nick found?

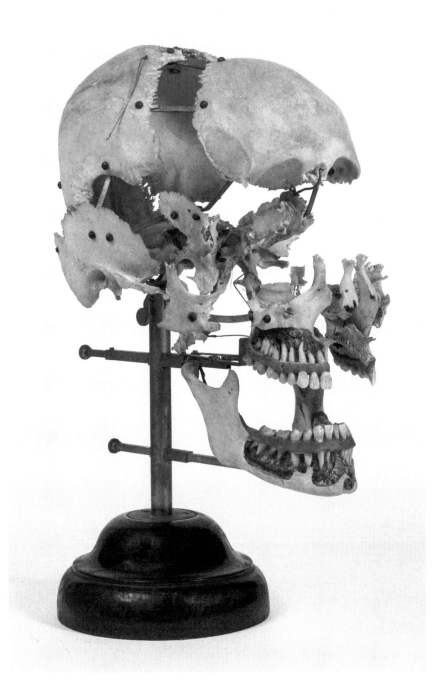

THE
EXPLODED SKULL

A very young Ryan in a devil costume
with his father, Stan

SKULLS OF THE FOREST
Ryan

I 've always been fascinated with death.

When I was a little kid, I'd wander around the woods behind my house. I grew up in upstate Maine and loved to go exploring in nature. I would find all kinds of fascinating natural specimens: bird feathers, dead beetles, animal bones. Instead of just admiring these objects, I felt compelled to keep them. I would bring them home with me and put them in various boxes that I kept under my bed.

Sometimes I'd drag my specimens out of their hiding place and lay them out on the floor so I could look at them. To someone from the city or the suburbs, that might seem a little creepy, but I was fascinated with nature. When you live in a rural area, death is part of the natural cycle of life. My interest in dead things wasn't considered strange or odd by my parents or friends (though my little sister was a bit creeped out by the stuff she'd find when she went snooping in my room). It was a fairly normal part of growing up in the woods. I was only five or six years old, but I was already creating my own little world underneath my bed.

My parents had a pretty significant library, and one of my favorite books was an encyclopedia that had detailed diagrams of human anatomy. It started with the skeletal system, and then I'd turn the page, which was completely clear, and lay the muscular system on top of it. The next page had the vascular system with all the blood vessels, and then the nervous system came next. In this manner I could put together the human body so I could see what we looked like underneath our skin.

I was obsessed with those diagrams of the body. Flipping back and forth through the pages was like watching someone decompose and then spring back to life. Mostly I used the book as a reference for

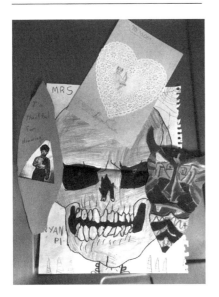

Ryan was destined to become an oddity. His art at age six had all the telltale signs . . .

my drawings. I'd slide the book off its shelf and keep it in my room. My mom was always yelling at me. "Hey, there's an encyclopedia missing!" When I admitted to having it, she'd tell me to put it back, and I would, only to bring the book up to my room again a week or two later.

My parents didn't worry about me or think I was a weirdo even though I was holed up in my room drawing skeletons all the time or foraging through the woods looking for specimens. I wasn't mean or cruel. I was always very compassionate with creatures big and small. I didn't have a violent bone in my body. In fact, I was afraid of the dark and profoundly claustrophobic—and I remain so to this day.

My parents thought my fascination with anatomy and death was a good thing. *Maybe little Ryan will become a doctor.* I think that was their hope—at least early on. They were definitely supportive. I found out many years later that my interest in this stuff was neither strange nor unique. There was a huge group of people out there who loved natural history as much as I did. I just hadn't found them yet.

When I was about twelve years old, I started to make things. It was a natural extension of my interest in anatomy and in the objects I found in the woods. I'd make little sculptures out of bones, broken dolls, and natural specimens. That's when I really started to delve into the intersection of art and anatomy. I was already making paintings and drawings, but now I was adding the things I found in the woods, arranging the material in particular ways. I guess you could call what I was doing "mixed-media collage," but I didn't know back then that there was a name for it. Making art was just something I did because I was interested in it and liked the way the objects looked together.

Even when I got to the point where I understood I was making art, I wasn't interested in doing anything with the pieces I created. I wasn't trying to sell these works or show them off. I just thought they looked cool, and I felt compelled to make more.

As I started to refine my skills, I became interested in putting my own skeletons together, whatever that might mean. I didn't have much money, so I kept foraging in the woods, collecting all kinds of different things in the hopes of being able to make art out of the materials I found. The desire to put together a complete skeleton was very strong, and I realized I wasn't going to find everything I was looking for in the forest. I needed to expand my search.

As a young collector, I didn't have a lot of funds. The only resource I had was searching for images online or in the local library. I did as much research as I could. You have to keep in mind that this was during the mid '90s, when the internet was still relatively new to the general public. The World Wide Web was nothing like it is today. I really had to dig deep to find anything of value.

I somehow stumbled upon an image of an exploded skull. I found the website of an artist who had gone to numerous natural history museums around the world and photographed various disarticulated skulls. I didn't know anything about the process for "exploding" a skull. All I knew was that it was incredibly attractive to me as an artist. I wanted to figure out how I could turn my specimens into something that was arresting to the eye and aesthetically appealing. I was completely taken by the beauty of exploded skulls.

Most people think the human skull is made up of two bones: the cranium and the jawbone. Actually, the human skull has twenty-two bones. There are eight cranial bones and fourteen facial bones. An exploded skull is when you separate, or disarticulate, these bones at the sutures and mount them on armatures so that it looks like the bones of the skull are flying away from one another.

It's actually called a Beauchêne skull because the process of disarticulating the human skull supposedly began with the French doctor Edmé François Chauvot de Beauchêne. Although the earliest drawings of a disarticulated skull go all the way back to the sixteenth century via Leonardo da Vinci, it was Beauchêne who actually created the first medical model of a disarticulated skull. These models were used by doctors and medical professionals to study all of the intricacies of the cranium. With a disarticulated skull, they could see a cross section of the skull and both the interior of the cranium and the exterior of the facial bones. For the first time, the temporal bone, the occipital bone, and all the pieces of the skull were viewable in three dimensions. Instead of looking at one single entity, the exploded skull made it possible to see each individual bone.

My research led me to the existence of medical museums. In the '90s, most museums weren't putting their collections online. They used the internet like glorified yellow pages. I started calling up the museums I found online, asking all kinds of questions about exploded skulls. That's when I discovered the Mütter Museum at the College of Physicians of Philadelphia.

Dr. Thomas Dent Mütter was a nineteenth-century physician and surgeon who was dedicated to expanding the knowledge of medical professionals. When he died, he left his collection of medical instruments and specimens, and a large sum of money, for the creation of a museum. The first building was completed in 1863, and the museum has expanded over the years. Today, it has over twenty-five thousand objects, including a few examples of Beauchêne skulls.

When I was in my early teens, my family moved to Woodstock in upstate New York, which made it easier for me and my three siblings—my older brother Shaun, my younger brother Evan, and my little sister Jennifer—to take trips into New York City, where I became completely enchanted with exploded skulls. There was just one problem: The museums didn't allow guests to take photographs. I always brought my sketchbook with me, so I sat down on the floor and drew the exploded skulls on display as best I could to figure out how these things were put together.

I was fascinated with the way the skulls were displayed, which is something that has stayed with me all my life. I always pay careful attention not only to the objects in my collection but to how they are presented.

A skull is a skull. Everyone knows what skulls look like. The presentation is what makes a Beauchêne skull preparation beautiful and unique. Without the armature supporting the individual pieces and making them appear to be floating, all you've got is a pile of bones. When it's done right, the pieces of the skull seem to hover in the air as if by magic, providing new ways to study the cranium. This was useful for early anatomists who wanted to learn how the pieces of the skull fit together, but my obsession went deeper than that. I wanted to know how the display was constructed so that I could replicate the process myself. Before I could figure out how to put the pieces of a skull together, I had to learn how to take them apart.

I found an article online from a scientist at Yale who discussed the process of disarticulating a skull, and I decided to give it a try. I printed out everything I could find about exploded skulls, which was mostly photos I'd found online. There wasn't a field guide or a YouTube tutorial for this sort of thing back then.

My first attempt, on a vervet monkey skull, was kind of a disaster. I bought the skull online from a collector who lived in Florida. Once I had the skull ready to go, the next step was to prepare the gelatin, which is a microbiological agar. It's basically no different from the Jell-O that you can buy in the store except that it's clear and unflavored. Once the gelatin was prepared, I filled the skull with it and put it in the freezer. As the gelatin froze, it expanded, pushing the plates of the skull apart until the sutures that knit them together came loose and the bones were completely disarticulated.

That was the easy part. Mounting the bones on metal armatures and putting the pieces back together again was another matter. Because I didn't know what I was doing, the assembly process was incredibly time consuming and a lot more challenging than I thought it would be. Each piece of metal had to be custom cut, drilled, and tapped so that a screw could be held securely. Every obstacle seemed insurmountable.

I quickly discovered that I didn't have the right tools. It turns out there's a special holder that frees up the hands and makes this kind of work much easier. Also, the drill I was using was too big and heavy for such delicate work. It was all trial and error, and I made plenty of errors.

For instance, if you drill too big of a hole in the bone or jostle the screw around too much, it becomes loose. Out of necessity, I secured the pieces that had come loose with glue. When I was done, I was disappointed with my efforts. The skull looked okay, but upon closer inspection anyone could see it was shabbily put together. I knew the glue wouldn't stand the test of time. I needed more practice.

The next preparation I did turned out better. The second skull belonged to an adult chacma baboon. It was slightly bigger and not as delicate as the monkey skull, but it took much more effort to pry the sutures apart. Once again, my preparation passed the eyeball test, but I was far from satisfied.

Around that time I started taking trips to New York City on my own and was hanging around the Evolution Store on Broadway over by New York University. Evolution was known for selling antiques and anatomical specimens of the highest quality, but they also sold medical supplies, including human skulls and bones, which is legal in New York, as it is in most states. Before the advance of computers, medical students used actual skulls to study anatomy.

Skulls have been a source of fascination for students, scientists, scholars, and artists for centuries. They symbolize everything we do not know about the human experience: the workings of the brain, the mystery of consciousness, and what happens to us after death. I was fortunate to get into osteological art at a time when there were strict prohibitions on the types of skulls that could be purchased. I say "fortunate" because it helped me understand early on that there's a right way of doing things and a wrong way. Of course, procuring skulls from graves was forbidden, and the Native American Graves Protection and Repatriation Act, which was passed in 1990, protected the human remains of Indigenous Americans. I'm grateful my mentors taught me to treat the skulls and skeletons of *all* creatures with respect and to always abide by the law. When less scrupulous collectors take shortcuts and ignore the law, they cause a great deal of harm, and the media has a tendency to paint all collectors of oddities with the same brush.

I was focused on antique medical specimens, and Evolution had a beautiful nineteenth-century French Beauchêne skull on display that I became obsessed with. The price was between $15,000 and $20,000, which seemed astronomical to me at the time.

A guy named Ryan who worked at Evolution did all the articulations that were sold in the store. He was the expert, and he taught me a great deal. He actually let me photograph the Beauchêne skull. I started asking Ryan all kinds of questions about creating exploded skulls. Ryan was patient and thorough, and he treated the artifacts under his care with the utmost respect. When he thought I was ready, he sold me a medical-grade skull of antiquity from his personal collection that had already been disarticulated. Each of the skull's bones was numbered. All I had to do was put it back together again.

"Here you go," he said. "Good luck."

The skull didn't cost nearly as much as it would today because there wasn't a lot of interest in articulating skulls at that time. That's no longer the case, which is partially my fault. Nevertheless, at the time a skull purchased through a company like Evolution would have cost several thousand dollars. This was a serious investment for a young artist like me. If I cracked a piece of the skull or messed up the display, then I ruined something that cost an awful lot of money.

My first human exploded skull came out pretty well. That inspired me to keep at it. As I acquired better tools and accumulated more knowledge and experience, I began to refine my process. In the beginning, I made every single part of the armature by hand. I was basically starting from scratch with each piece. I eventually learned to cast different parts so that I didn't have to go through the process of making each individual piece. Now I can cast four or five pieces at a time, which makes the process a lot faster.

It was a long, slow journey, but I was starting to figure things out. My pieces were not only beautiful to look at but sturdy and strong. Some of the skulls I've done in more recent years are so well put together you can drop them on the floor and they will stay intact.

From skulls, I worked my way up to skeletons, which had been my ambition all along. The first skeleton I put together was a wallaby from Australia that I bought from Ryan at Evolution. He showed me the ropes and gave me some useful tips, but there's only so much you can learn without actually getting in there and doing it yourself. You learn by doing. I studied diagrams and attempted to replicate what I saw. Trying to match the sections of the vertebrae or figuring out which toe bone went where was like trying to assemble an intricate puzzle. I made some mistakes with the smaller bones, especially the really delicate ones. I thought the wallaby would be easy, but I was wrong.

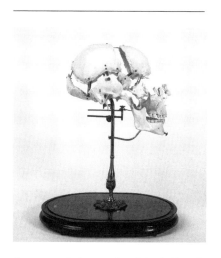

The finished piece looked okay, but I knew that it was deeply flawed. I kept it for a while because the wallaby was my first articulation, but it was destroyed when one of the shelves in my bedroom fell, smashing the skeleton to pieces on the floor.

From that point on, I was hooked. I devoted all of my free time and energy to osteological art. That's all I did. I would

A very pristine and original French nineteenth-century exploded skull that was the inspiration for many of Ryan's osteological creations

save up my money, and when an antique skull or an animal skeleton became available, I would buy it. I would stay up all night working on these pieces, just drinking coffee and hardly sleeping. It was really important to me to get the process right so that if an expert appraised my work, they would see not only that it looked beautiful but that it had been done correctly.

Once I was old enough to move to Brooklyn and have a little apartment of my own, I was finally able to display my pieces as art. That's when I started to think of them as a collection. I didn't have the money to buy pieces of osteological art, so I learned how to make them myself. I transformed a tiny area in my apartment into a makeshift studio where I could work on preparations—and when I was finished with a piece, I would put it on display. That's where it all started for me.

When I wasn't preparing a new piece, I was conducting research on the computer or out in the field. I'd go to museums and take pictures or go to libraries and ask all kinds of questions. I would get up in the middle of the night and take the train into Manhattan from Brooklyn to go to flea markets. I would be the first one there when they opened, and I would hang out waiting for vendors to put things out. Even when I didn't buy anything, those early-morning excursions took my collecting to a whole new level and added to the feeling that I was on an adventure. There wasn't one aspect of collecting that I loved more than others; I embraced all of it.

The four flea markets that I usually went to in the city were all in roughly the same area, from around 23rd Street up to 25th Street. There was one called the Garage and another one just outside of it where I would always find stuff. There was another market across the street, but you had to pay $1 to get into it. Then there was the "derelict" market around the block. It was called that because there were always drug addicts and thieves looking to sell stuff, most of which had clearly been stolen. These were the four big markets that were open every Saturday and Sunday.

You would think that a Manhattan flea market would be a poor place to look for an animal skeleton or an osteological rarity, and you would be wrong. I found the craziest things at these markets. I went most weekends, and if I didn't go to one of those four, there was also a market down on 11th Street and Avenue A right near Tompkins Square Park at the basketball court. That was a neighborhood market, and you could get a table to sell at for just $12. The pickings were slim there, but the prices tended to be better. I never knew what I was going to find. Many of the Lower East Side artists would sell items from their apartments at this market to make extra money. It was like a yard sale for eccentrics. There were even rumors that people would find original Robert Mapplethorpe photographs and Keith Haring paintings for very little money—and then sell those pieces at auction for millions.

I figured out that I could have a great-looking oddities collection by doing many of the preparations myself. I became really intimate with the science and the know-how behind making exploded skulls and articulated skeletons look beautiful. Some collectors love acquiring things, and others obsess about possessing objects that no one else has. I like those aspects too, but for me the best moment is when the piece is ready to be put on display with the rest of my collection. For me, the presentation is the point. Otherwise I'm just a hoarder. From the very beginning, I started to think of my little apartment as a pseudomuseum.

THE CZAR OF CARDS
Ryan

Once I started collecting oddities, there was no looking back, but it wasn't my first business endeavor. I already had considerable experience buying and selling in the collectibles marketplace.

When I was a kid, I was completely obsessed with baseball cards. I was fascinated by how much these little bits of cardboard were worth and why they were so valuable. I figured out that if I bought a batch of baseball cards, I could pick out the ones that were valuable and sell them for more money than I had paid for the entire lot. That was my introduction to the business side of collecting.

It didn't take me long to figure out how the baseball card business worked, and I started dealing in pieces that were worth a crazy amount of money for a little kid. When I was twelve years old, I was finding Mickey Mantle rookie cards and trading tobacco cards (cards produced by the tobacco industry in the late nineteenth and early twentieth centuries). My mom would drop me off at the baseball card shop, and I would negotiate my own deals. She wouldn't even come into the store with me. I was so obsessed that my friends and family gave me baseball cards for my bar mitzvah. Baseball cards were better than cash because I could trade them for cards that were even more valuable.

I kept acquiring more cards until I had a pretty substantial collection. At its peak, I had hundreds of thousands of baseball cards in my possession. My whole room was packed with boxes and boxes of cards. A family friend in Florida was also sending me autographed baseballs. He installed the water pipes at professional baseball fields and would regularly ask players for autographs. My room looked like a sports card store. The funny thing was I absolutely hated sports, especially baseball. I had no interest in it and found the actual game incredibly boring. To this day, I have never sat through an entire baseball game.

Despite my lack of interest, my parents made me play sports each year. My older brother, Shaun, was not only the captain of the football team but also the head of the wrestling team. As a result, one year my father encouraged me to join the wrestling team, which I didn't want to do because I was smaller than the other kids and uninterested in athletics. During my first meet, because there weren't any other boys in my weight class, they made me wrestle a girl. I'm not exaggerating when I say she kicked the shit out of me. She even gave me a bloody lip. I remember there was a girl I liked at school, and she came to watch my match that day. Needless to say, getting my ass handed to me by a girl didn't help my chances with my crush.

There was always this interesting juxtaposition between my passion for collecting baseball cards and my complete lack of interest in the sport. I didn't watch the game. I didn't have a favorite team. I didn't play it as a kid. My passion for collecting cards had nothing to do with the game itself.

I believe this made me a better collector. Because I didn't have a sentimental attachment to a particular player or team, it was easy for me to let the cards go. I didn't have any hang-ups about holding on to certain cards. By trading up, I was able to improve the quality of my collection. This was an extremely valuable lesson that I would carry with me to all of my business dealings for the rest of my collecting career. No matter how rewarding it is to collect things that you're passionate about, if you want your collection to grow, you have to be willing to let things go.

I was introduced to collecting baseball cards by some of my friends at school. They were really into it, and I wanted to see what all the fuss was about, but this wasn't the first time my friends turned me on to a lucrative business opportunity. I was always looking for ways to make a little extra money to buy supplies for my weird little art projects.

For instance, the kids at my school went through a phase where they were really into toothpicks. Shaun and I figured out how to make cinnamon-flavored toothpicks. We'd make little packs of them and sell them at school, which was against school rules. For a minute, toothpicks became a big deal at our school. We were basically dealing them like drugs.

We never got caught, but eventually the fad wore out. Nothing stays popular forever—another valuable lesson. Kids stopped buying toothpicks, and we moved on to the next thing. For a while, Evan and I sold fake cigarettes that we made at home. These "cigarettes" weren't meant to be smoked. The "tobacco" was made out of ground-up leaves that we found in the forest, mixed with various spices from my mother's cupboard. We'd put the cigarettes in old playing card boxes and design them so they looked like a real pack of cigarettes. They were purely decorative, but the kids liked them. We sold those fake packs of cigarettes and made a little money. In retrospect, we were probably encouraging underage smoking, but we didn't look at it that way since we were also underage.

I got my eye for business opportunities from my father, who loved old, rare cars. If he saw an old car that needed a little TLC, he'd buy it, have it fixed up, and drive it around until another car caught his attention. Then he'd sell the first car at a handsome profit and start the process all over again. The funny thing was he didn't know all that much about cars—he just liked driving them around and showing them off. He would hire people to fix them up for him. For my dad, the cars were an investment, but it wasn't just about the money. He genuinely loved those old cars and had a lot of fun driving them. You can't do that with a stamp collection.

My mania for baseball cards was an extension of my dad's entrepreneurial impulse. I learned the value of investing in things that appreciated in value over time. I think my fixation on presentation stems from a desire to enjoy the pieces of my collection for their aesthetic beauty and not stuff them in a box in the back of the closet. My dad taught me that I can be a savvy collector and have fun doing it. I make sure to enjoy my items, but I always remember that they are an investment. Eventually, I must be willing to sell them to make a profit.

In my late teens, I sold my entire baseball collection to a card collector in the city. I think I made something like $18,000 on that sale, which at the time was a lot of money for me. In fact, it funded my move to my own apartment in Brooklyn after I graduated from high school.

Buying and selling baseball cards taught me how to play the game. I knew I was good at buying low and selling high. I cultivated an eye for things that increased in value and developed a knack for knowing when to sell. Just like in real estate, timing is everything. The opportunity that presents itself today may be gone tomorrow. That's true for buyers *and* sellers. The most important thing about selling my cards was that it gave me confidence. I knew that if I did it once, I could do it again.

When I got into buying and selling oddities, I'd already learned that it wasn't the size of the collection that mattered, but the quality of the individual pieces. So when I started collecting osteological artifacts, I was constantly trading up, selling items in my collection for pieces that were higher quality, harder to find, or more unique. Eventually, I started acquiring pieces I had no interest in keeping for myself. I'd buy artifacts that I knew I could sell for a profit so I could buy the things I really wanted.

You have to know how to play the game if you want to survive in the business. You have to know the value of things. You have to be able to make split decisions that can change your life in an instant. If you're not spontaneous, you miss the opportunity forever. You can't stop time and think it over, weighing the pros and cons. That's not how this business works.

The most important thing of all is that you have to develop relationships. The person you buy from today might be someone you sell to tomorrow (and vice versa). People need to trust in your expertise and count on you to do the right thing. That trust is the backbone of everything we do.

ODD JOBS
Ryan

I needed a job.

In my twenties, I was dating a woman who was doing computer work for an old guy named Arnold Goldstein. He was one of the very first people to work for Ralph Lauren back when he was making ties in the Empire State Building in the late '60s. Lauren got his start with neckwear, and then he expanded the business into the monster that it is today.

Early in his career, Lauren would incorporate designs inspired by Western wear into the preppy look that he was known for, which ended up becoming his signature style. Lauren hired Goldstein to be his jewelry maker, and he did all kinds of custom work in silver, other metals, and occasionally leather. Goldstein was a jack-of-all-trades who had many skills. There was no one better at making distressed leather look very, very old.

Goldstein's claim to fame was that he was Ralph Lauren's first designer. He must have been at least seventy years old when I started working for him—maybe even older than that.

I was young and still finding my way. I was living in Bushwick, Brooklyn, and trying to make a go of things, making art and building my collection. In addition to osteological art and other curiosities, I was starting to get into playing music and was developing an interest in guitars and tattoos. I had all these expensive hobbies and needed some steady income to make sure I could pay my bills at the end of the month.

I'd never had a conventional job before I started working with Goldstein. In fact, I didn't have any experience working with others. The job paid $10 an hour, and at that point in my life, that seemed like really good money.

Goldstein's studio was in Manhattan above the Garage flea market on 24th Street. He lived right above it on the third floor, which I thought was cool. He had the whole floor of this loft apartment, and it was filled with tools, antiques, sculptures, and prototypes that he'd done for Ralph Lauren over the decades. One little room was set up with antique French leather club chairs from the 1920s and looked really nice, but his bedroom, like every other room, looked like a workshop and was filled with all of these cool old tools.

The loft was divided into workstations. He had an area to work on turquoise, an area to work on sterling silver, an area to work on assembling things. The station that I typically inhabited was where we did all the grinding, soldering, and metalworking.

For the first year I worked for Goldstein, I absolutely hated him because he made me do the same thing every day. I started at nine o'clock and would sit there and grind out an order for hours and hours. Sometimes it was twenty-five pieces. Sometimes it was 150. I didn't have a set quitting time. I worked until the orders were finished. Grind and polish, grind and polish, all day long.

Sometimes I would do some refined metalwork with precision tools. Sometimes I would solder. Then it was literally back to the grind. I worked five days a week and had the weekends off.

It was tedious, repetitive work that reminded me of the movie *The Karate Kid*, where Ralph Macchio's character, Daniel, is like, "Mr. Miyagi, what the fuck? I feel like I'm just doing your chores!" and then came the day when he learned that he actually knew how to do karate from all of his "training." It was very similar to what I was doing, but I'm getting ahead of myself.

After about a year of working for Goldstein, I got my hand stuck in a machine. The job was starting to feel like a liability. I didn't want to lose my hand and become a moody, tormented artist like Nicolas Cage in *Moonstruck*. I was ready to quit the workshop because I was sick of doing the same thing over and over again. I confronted Goldstein and told him how I felt.

"I'm not learning anything," I complained. "I'm doing the same thing every day!"

Goldstein took me into his room and said, "What do you want to learn?"

"I want to learn how to assemble my own pieces," I said.

I had ideas about taking the sculptures I made out of bone and other found objects and making jewelry out of them.

"Okay," he said, "give me the components."

As Goldstein showed me how he assembled his pieces, I realized he'd been teaching me all the steps I needed all along. I already knew everything I needed to know about manipulating metal, I just had to apply what I'd learned to my own vision. I went from hating this man to realizing he'd given me an invaluable education. I'd learned more about precision metalworking in one year working for Goldstein than if I had gone to college or art school.

That realization unlocked a deeper understanding of the art of metalworking. I learned how to take natural elements like bone, stones, and coral and apply the principles of metalworking to them. This also had direct applications in the repairs and restorations I was doing with antiques. If I found something that was damaged, I now had the skills to restore it to its former grandeur and sell it at a substantial profit. I got to the point where I could take anything apart, then put it back together, and it would be better than it was before.

I always say that Goldstein taught me like a ninja. He was hard on me and he could be stingy in his praise, but under his tutelage I took my metalworking skills up a notch.

I stayed on for a few more years, learning everything I could from him. It was actually one of the only jobs I've ever had for any length of time in my entire life. Sometimes it was a lot of fun. If he was out of town, he'd let me stay in his loft so I could get a jump on the flea market below his apartment when it opened.

I guess you could call it an apprenticeship that I got paid for, but he enabled me to achieve the kind of quality craftsmanship to which I'd always aspired. That expertise quickly translated to the pieces I created or restored and took my career to the next level.

There was a company in the nineteenth century called Tramond of Paris that sold medical preparations, including disarticulated skulls. It was not uncommon to see these medical-grade skulls come up for auction from time to time. When I was starting out, I would use these as models for the exploded skulls that I created. After working for Goldstein, my craftmanship was on a par with the skulls created by Tramond of Paris.

I was moving up, but I was far from satisfied.

CHAPTER II

THE
KAPALA

Regina from her days at Agent Provocateur on Madison Avenue, NYC

EVOLUTION
Ryan

Evolution was hugely important to my understanding and appreciation of osteological art. That's where I saw my first kapala. A kapala is a Tibetan vessel fashioned from a skull, skullcap, or shell. These objects are used in Buddhist and Hindu Tantra traditions for a variety of purposes, including meditation, religious rituals, and funerary practices. What makes these objects so visually striking is that they are often ornamented with precious metals and stones, such as coral, turquoise, quartz, and onyx.

Sometimes a kapala will feature the entire skull or just a piece of it, like the skullcap, that is intricately carved and decorated with gems and jewels. Kapalas had many purposes and were used as receptacles for ceremonial objects or even as drinking bowls. These were typically lined with copper, silver, or brass and would sit on stands that were made of the same materials.

The kapala that Evolution had on display was a skull that had been decorated with turquoise, coral, and other precious stones. I was blown away by the craftmanship of the piece but also by its aesthetic beauty. This was a work of osteological art that was far beyond

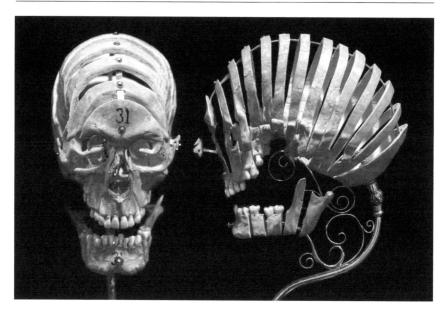

An original osteological concept created by Ryan. He sliced a skull into fourteen vertical sections. It was intended for people in the medical field to have the ability to study not only the interior but also the various cross sections of the skull.

anything I'd seen before. It was both decorative *and* symbolic, as opposed to the Beauchêne skulls that were created for educational and scientific purposes.

After seeing that first kapala skull, I began to notice them all over the place, which is usually how it goes. Once you become interested in something very specific, you start to see it everywhere. However, because of their beauty and the value of their gemstones, they were prohibitively expensive. I really wanted one, so I kept my eyes open, but I had to wait for the right opportunity.

The first example that I purchased was really beat up, which was why I was able to afford it. I got it from the flea market on 23rd and 24th Streets. It was decorated with beads, some of which were missing, and the metalwork was in rough shape. I thought if I could bring it up to par, I could add it to my collection.

The skills I had acquired creating exploded skulls helped me restore the kapala to its former glory, but I was limited by my inexperience. I had much more to learn. My thirst for knowledge about the pieces I was pursuing was a kind of substitute for acquiring them. If I couldn't find or afford the object in question, the next best thing was to learn everything I possibly could about it to prepare for when the opportunity presented itself.

I didn't "graduate" from making my own presentations of skeletons and skulls to pursuing kapalas. I was obsessed with osteological art in all its forms, and I built my reputation as an expert and maker of exploded skulls. It became something I was known for in collecting circles.

However, it was a kapala that had the greatest impact on my life. If it weren't for one very expensive kapala, I wouldn't have met Regina. She tells the story much better than I do, so I'll step aside, and she can take it from here.

———— ◆◆ ————

A KAPALA FOR CHRISTMAS
Regina

T he story of how I met Ryan begins with a skull.
    I was working for Agent Provocateur, a British fashion house that sold high-end lingerie. I managed the flagship store on Madison Avenue in New York City. The first year I worked there, we pulled in something like $7 million in sales, which was crazy. At the time, I was dating a gentleman who will remain nameless because he's a very well-known public figure, but I can tell you he's an actor and remains a very close friend.

Christmas was coming, and I had been watching Ryan's show *Oddities* on the Science Channel. I loved to stream the show in the background while I was cleaning the house or cooking dinner. I have to admit I would only really pay attention if I heard Ryan's voice come on. I started following Ryan on social media, and he would list objects he had that were for sale.

One day while I was at work, I noticed that he'd posted a photo of this beautiful Tibetan kapala skull that was silver and red and decorated with bits of coral. It wasn't like a medical school skull. This one was extremely blinged out. I thought it was beautiful.

I was interested in the piece, but the gentleman I was dating didn't understand my fascination with it. He was somewhat conflicted about the situation because Christmas was coming, and he wanted to get me something special.

"Do you really want *that* for Christmas? Is that *really* what you want?"

"Yes," I said.

"I *personally* would never want a human skull in the house," he said.

"*I* think it's gorgeous," I said.

"If that's really what you want for Christmas," he said, "I'll get it for you."

He was really adamant about not wanting to share space with a skull, but he also wanted to buy me something that was memorable and unique, something no one else had. It became this awkward thing between us.

Before I went any further, I decided to reach out to Ryan about the kapala. Ryan never put a price on the pieces he shared online; instead, he instructed those interested to message him privately for the price. I hesitantly messaged Ryan and left him my email address so he could get back to me. I asked him if it was still available, requested more details about the piece, and—most importantly—how much it cost.

Ryan wrote back almost immediately with the price and said it was mine if I wanted it. I was so excited! But my excitement quickly turned to dread when I saw that the cost was $6,000.

I felt embarrassed to tell the person I was dating how much it cost because even though he'd made such a big stink about the kapala, he said he was going to buy it for me for Christmas anyway. I knew there was no way I could accept such an expensive gift at that point in our relationship. In hindsight, that was the right move to make because the relationship didn't last long after that.

Ryan, however, now had my email address, and he quickly started to "clientele" me. Anytime Ryan had an expensive new item for sale, he would send me an email with photos, a description, and a price, just to see if I was interested. It's good business practice, but it was more than that. I could tell he was interested in *me*.

We exchanged emails from time to time, just an innocent back-and-forth that led to some casual chitchat. Eventually, we were full-on flirting with each other and having deeper conversations. This went on for a couple of months, well into the new year. I was now officially single and going through a hard time with a sick parent back in Rhode Island. I shared some of those details with Ryan, and he was very supportive. He would always check in to see how I was doing and would keep me company via text during some long and sad train rides to see my family. Looking back, it was all very sweet and romantic.

Finally, Ryan got up the nerve to ask me out.

"Hey, we're both in Brooklyn. Why don't you come to my studio sometime, and then we can go for a drink?"

I was flattered by the attention, but I wasn't sure if I actually wanted to meet up with Ryan in person. It was important to me that he didn't think I was just one of his many fangirls.

So I asked around. Based on our social media, I knew we had mutual friends. I checked in with some people who knew him. One of my coworkers was also a fan of the show and claimed to know Ryan.

"He asked me out," I told her. "Do you think I should go out with him?"

"Definitely!" she said. "Ryan's great. We're really good friends. You have to hang out with him!"

I was leaning toward turning him down, but his friend's testimonial led me to reconsider meeting up with this total stranger.

I emailed Ryan and told him I'd meet him for a drink, but I made my intentions very clear. "Just so you know, this isn't a date. If you think this is a date, I don't think we should meet." We still laugh about this conversation to this day.

This was during the prime of Ryan's television show, *Oddities*. I didn't want him to think I was fangirling him, and I didn't want him to get the wrong idea about me. I was older than him, for one thing, and I had my own career. To be perfectly honest, I found his persona on social media kind of off-putting.

Ryan wrote back and said, "We'll chat, and I can tell you more about what I do for a living."

I agreed, and we planned to meet at a popular bar in Brooklyn. I was definitely a bit nervous, so I ordered a glass of wine to calm my nerves while I waited for him to arrive. He was a few minutes late because there was a bad rainstorm that night. He walked in, spotted me instantly, and headed over to where I was sitting. Within the first ten seconds of meeting him I accidentally insulted him. When I stood up to greet him, I blurted out, "Wow, you are much smaller in person."

I didn't mean to embarrass him. I wouldn't have blamed him if he had walked right out, but he didn't. He stayed. I was wearing 4-inch heels, so I guess he wasn't *that* short.

He laughed it off and followed it up with, "Have you ever seen a man with two penises?"

He then whipped out his phone and started showing me an article he had just read that included some very descriptive photos. I realized my comment didn't faze him in the least, and I knew we were going to get along just fine.

We had a drink, which led to dinner with a lot more red wine. From there we decided to go across the street to another bar and have even more cocktails. By the end of the night, I already felt we were connected.

We never did make it over to his studio that evening. As for the woman who claimed to be such good friends with Ryan? It turns out they barely knew each other.

After our first meeting, we started texting each other, and for our second meeting we went on a

Ryan and Regina early in their relationship

proper date to see a movie. He gave me a beautiful sterling silver and gold skull pendant that he'd spent all day making, and I brought him a box of pineapple gummy bears because he mentioned they were his favorite. As small a gesture as that might seem, I had to go all the way to Manhattan to Dylan's Candy Bar to get them. It still makes me laugh that he gave me fine jewelry, and I gave him a bag of sugar.

On our third date, we said "I love you" over dinner at a Japanese restaurant. It was a whirlwind romance, which was somewhat shocking to our friends and family, who'd never seen us act this way before.

Shortly afterward, I left Agent Provocateur and started a job with a Parisian fashion company. I was overseeing the whole northeast and was responsible for over a hundred stores. I was traveling around the country and flying out to Paris just about every other month. Ryan would sometimes accompany me on my travels if it was a cool city, but he never missed those Paris trips. He'd roam around the city, searching for antiques and oddities while I worked. Then when I was done for the day, we'd go explore museums and hunt for inspiration together. It was all very romantic.

On one of those occasions, barely six months after we met, Ryan flew out to meet me in Paris. Because flying can trigger Ryan's claustrophobia, he'd taken a Xanax so he could sleep on the plane. As a result, he wasn't in great shape when he landed. When he arrived at the hotel, he carelessly threw his bag on the bed and a ring box rolled out onto the floor.

I thought, *Is that what I think it is? Is he really going to propose to me in Paris?*

I acted like I didn't see it, and he put the ring away without realizing that I'd spotted it.

The next morning we went to the Catacombs of Paris, which were amazing. I had no idea that up until fairly recently, throughout Europe, burying someone in the ground was just the first step in the body's journey. After the flesh decomposed, the bones were often dug up and taken to an ossuary, which was the final resting place for large numbers of skeletal remains.

Ryan insisted that we visit. It was an odd choice—not because it's an underground ossuary that is home to millions of skulls but because of Ryan's severe claustrophobia. The catacombs are very deep below the city streets, and by the time we got to the bottom, Ryan was pale, sweating, and acting a little erratic.

At one point, he kept pointing to a particular cracked skull, wanting me to look inside it, which I really didn't want to do. Ryan was weirdly insistent. I was sure there was a rat or some other creature inside the skull, so I was reluctant to approach. It slowly dawned on me why Ryan *really* wanted me to look at it, and when I finally did, I noticed the ring box inside.

Ryan clumsily got down on one knee, but it was so dark I couldn't see exactly what he was doing.

That's when he popped the question.

"Will you marry me?"

"Uh, yes?" I said.

Ryan must have been in really bad shape with his claustrophobia because as soon as I accepted his proposal, he stood up and essentially ran out of the catacombs as fast as he could. He basically left me in the dust. I remember there was an older woman on the stairs who was moving really slowly, and Ryan literally squeezed past her, which she wasn't too happy about.

When I caught up to Ryan aboveground, he was feeling much better. We wanted to take photos of the ring on my finger, but my nails were not up to par for such a special announcement. We walked into the first nail salon we could find so I could get a manicure.

It was anything but your typical storybook romance—and we owe it all to a hundred-year-old Tibetan kapala skull. Whoever you were and wherever you are, thank you!

———•••———

THE MISSIONARY'S UNDERWEAR
Regina

The first time I went on a buying trip with Ryan, we ended up purchasing a huge collection of artifacts, but that's not what made the trip so memorable. There was a problem: All the pieces were wrapped in men's underwear.

Ryan received an email from a fan, which in most cases usually doesn't lead to anything of substantial value. The emails we receive are mostly fan mail, and if there is an offer of goods, it's often something that's weird or illegal or just plain wrong—like the time a girl wanted to know if she could donate her body to us after she died. That was strange, but what made it even weirder was that she was very young, like fourteen. We wrote back, saying essentially, "Thanks but no thanks. Also, hopefully you live much longer than we do!"

This email was different. This particular young woman reached out to us because her father had recently passed away and had left behind a large number of osteological artifacts. She wanted to know if we were interested in purchasing the entire collection.

"You have first dibs if you want to come out to Alabama!" she wrote.

She sent over a handful of photographs, and right away we could tell it was an impressive collection. The artifacts weren't professionally photographed. These were snapshots taken on a camera phone, but we could see what looked like skullcaps carved with intricate designs. That told us we were looking at Tibetan kapalas.

Ryan wrote back to her: "I want everything."

"When can you come?" she asked.

"I'll be there tomorrow."

I was still working in my fashion career at the time, but I wanted to go with Ryan on this trip because I had never gone on a buying trip before, and it seemed like so much fun.

"I'm going with you," I told him.

Ryan couldn't tell if I was serious. "Really?"

"I'll take a couple of days off," I said, "because I really want to see what you do."

KAPALA MATERIALS

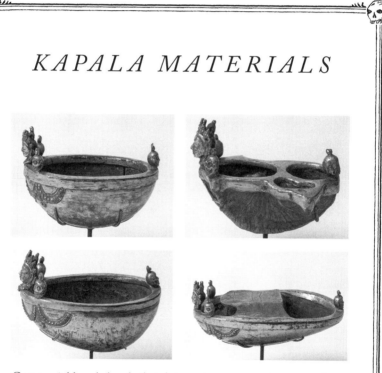

Ceremonial kapala bowls that date to the seventeenth century from Nepal. Made from materials such as coconut, nautilus, skull, and turtle shell.

So the next day we flew to see her collection. The woman lived in a condominium with her new husband. They were both really young; if I had to guess, I'd say early twenties. She had all of these boxes out in her living room that she had taken from her dad's place when he passed. After a bit of chitchat, we anxiously started going through the boxes, and it was really awkward because every single item was wrapped in used underwear.

Mind you, I was working for a lingerie company at the time, so I'm not a prude by any means, but this was not nice underwear. It belonged to the young woman's deceased father, and they were your basic Hanes tighty-whities. The underpants were clean, but they were old and dingy and full of holes—and incredibly large. I'm not sure "large" quite paints the picture. If I'm being honest, they were enormous!

We didn't want to be rude because we were unwrapping the items right in front of the woman who'd invited us into her home and who had recently lost her father, but it was very uncomfortable. I really wished she had given us some rubber gloves first.

Once I got past the fact that I was unraveling items wrapped in underwear, it was obvious that this was a once-in-a-lifetime collection. It contained well over one hundred pieces, and each kapala was more breathtaking than the last. This was a collection of items the likes of which we would never see again.

The young woman's father had been a missionary, which was not that uncommon. Missionaries would travel to foreign countries for service work and bring mementos back as reminders of the work they did in other communities. Back in the '50s, '60s, and '70s, people would go to developing countries and bring back all kinds of things. It was much easier to get archaeological artifacts into the United States back then. These missionaries would pick up an elongated skull from Peru, bring it back on the plane, and no one ever said a word. As strange as it sounds, Christian missionaries are responsible for the popularity of all kinds of oddities, including mummies and shrunken heads.

Because we'd just hopped on a plane without making any plans, Ryan had to go out and buy a ton of boxes and shipping supplies so we could safely send everything back home. He also bought bubble wrap so we could leave the missionary's underwear behind.

We spent the night packaging up the items. There were about 125 pieces when all was said and done. I asked Ryan if we should take any of it with us in our suitcase or carry-on bag. Ryan was dead set against that. He's a stickler for the rules and knows them inside and out—sometimes better than the TSA agents. He didn't want us or the objects to get held up at the airport because a TSA agent had never seen a kapala before.

One time we were out in California, and an artist friend I looked up to gifted me a monkey skull necklace. We were already at the airport when he gave it to me, so there was no time to ship it.

"Don't be afraid," he said. "Just wear it. No one's going to say anything."

It was a very special piece ornamented with feathers and bones. There was no way I was leaving it behind. I was determined to bring it home with me.

So I did. I just went for it. I knew there was a risk, but I decided that if they take it, they take it, but I'm gonna rock this thing through the airport and hold my head up high. Even though it wasn't something I normally did, I wore the necklace with the rest of my jewelry when we went through airport security.

Ryan was shaking in his proverbial boots. He didn't know exactly what breed of monkey it was. He was unsure where the feathers came from. He didn't know if it was a tribal piece, where it was from, or whether it was even technically allowed in the country. He didn't know those important details, and that made him nervous.

Whenever Ryan buys an artifact, he typically ships it home through the mail just to make sure that everything is kosher. He's very "by the book" in that regard, but on this occasion we didn't have time to even think about it.

I went for it, and my friend was right. I made it through just fine. No one said a thing about my monkey skull.

Back in Alabama, the young woman took us out to Denny's for breakfast in the morning, and she told us stories about her father. It had been some time since he had passed. During the breakfast, fans of Ryan kept coming up to our table, interrupting and asking for photos and autographs. In the end, we bought the collection for five figures and sold most of the pieces off individually.

The young woman had no interest in holding on to her father's collection. That's the way it usually goes—especially when it comes to oddities. She was just thrilled that somebody she looked up to was taking her dad's stuff off her hands—even though it was wrapped in his giant underpants!

THE MYSTERIOUS SARCOPHAGUS
Ryan

When I'm on a buying trip, things don't always go as planned. Although this book is full of successful deals, in fact many deals fall apart. Some go south in the beginning because the sellers misrepresent themselves or the objects they're trying to unload on me. Some deals don't pan out because I don't pull the trigger quickly enough. Although I'm always on the hunt, I don't buy just anything. I believe in value over volume, and I always try to do my homework. There are an infinite number of ways for a deal to go wrong, but occasionally not only do things go right, but I get more than I bargained for.

I'll buy anything I think is odd, old, interesting, or valuable. People reach out to me online all the time, but nothing beats dealing with people in person. I especially like doing business with experienced antiquarians who are knowledgeable about their area of expertise. I've been lucky to befriend a lot of curators, dealers, anthropologists, and other specialists—people who deal with antiquities on a professional level. These are the people I want to speak to and learn from when I'm researching a particular subject.

When I was living in Greenpoint, Brooklyn, I purchased an Egyptian sarcophagus that was originally in the possession of a university on Long Island and was later sold to a private collector. The sarcophagus had a fairly extensive paper trail that assured me that it had substantial provenance—but the contents were a mess. At one point, the sarcophagus had contained a mummy, but the skeleton had been disarticulated, and there was a jumble of bones, bitumen, and wrappings at the bottom of the coffin. As much as I wanted to go through the sarcophagus and reassemble the skeleton, I knew I was out of my element.

I reached out to a colleague who was an actual Egyptologist, and he agreed to examine the contents of the coffin with me. He was in high demand, and it was some time before he was able to come visit me in my studio. It was like having a Christmas present I wasn't able to unwrap. Finally, my scholarly friend arrived to inspect the sarcophagus with me.

The first thing we did was take out all of the objects and lay them on a table so we could inspect then, clean up any debris, and determine what was missing. Then we put the bones back into the sarcophagus where they belonged: The skull goes here, the torso goes there, etc. We worked our way down to the leg and toe bones. At the end of the exercise, we realized we had several extra bones.

For instance, this guy either had two right femurs or multiple mummies had been placed in this sarcophagus. While royal figures and members of wealthy families could afford to be buried alone, it wasn't uncommon for members of the same family to share a sarcophagus—especially if they weren't wealthy.

We also found several bundles of other remnants preserved in their wrappings, which I was reluctant to open for fear of damaging the contents. One small bundle caught my attention as a particularly good example of mummy wrappings of the period. I thought I would build a stand for it and add it to my collection, but it took me a while to get around to it.

About a year later, I was cleaning up my studio when I came across the bundle and inspected it more closely. This time I noticed a pinhole in the wrappings where part of the contents was exposed. Using a magnifying glass, I zoomed in on the pinhole and realized I was looking at a fingernail and the tip of a finger. I carefully unwrapped the bundle and made an astonishing discovery: a mummified hand.

I had this extremely rare and fascinating object in my possession for over a year without even knowing that it was there. It just goes to show that you never know what you'll find—even in your own collection.

CHAPTER III

THE SHRUNKEN HEAD

BILLY'S ANTIQUES

THE PROFESSOR'S COLLECTION

STOLEN OR NOT?

Ryan with the legendary Billy Leroy
and famed artist and collector Joe
Coleman

BILLY'S ANTIQUES
Ryan

The first shrunken head I purchased was from a really cool antique store called Billy's Antiques. It was on East Houston right off the Bowery in Manhattan, and it was a staple of that area of New York City. When I first started going to Billy's, there were still tons of antique stores, in the Lower East Side and all over New York City, but Billy's was unique, a legendary place.

It was one of the first antique stores I found when I moved to New York, and I remember my first thought when I set foot in the place: *How is this legal?*

Billy's Antiques was essentially a giant nylon tent. There were extension cords running everywhere, and it was heated with space heaters—a total fire hazard.

The guy who ran it was named Billy Leroy. We've became pretty good friends over the years, but in the beginning, we had something of a love-hate relationship. He was older than me, and he seemed to enjoy playing the role of mentor because I was curious about everything: what he knew, how he acquired objects, how he sold them. Billy taught me everything he knew until I knew just as much about certain things as he did—if not more.

Billy is 6 feet tall with a long ponytail and eyeglasses. There were two things I never saw Billy without: a cigar and a cane. He was a biker in a former life, and I think he actually needed the cane. It wasn't a fashion accessory. Like every other biker I've known, he had a bad back from riding motorcycles and had probably been in an accident or two.

What I found really cool about Billy was that from the first time I met him, he always wore a three-piece suit. No matter what he was doing, he was dressed in a vest and had on really nice shoes. He looked sharp and radiated cool. Billy was a legend on the Lower East Side.

Although we came to love and respect each other as friends and colleagues, we constantly butted heads. It was probably our competitive natures. He busted my chops all the time. It wasn't personal; it was just the way he was. I would try to give it right back to him, so there was always a lot of banter between the two of us when we were dealing together. We always tried to get the best of each other and wanted to come out on top.

I respected Billy because he was from the old school. He mostly dealt with a network of older collectors, some of whom had never even heard of the internet. In those days, the internet was wild and lawless. You could never trust that the objects listed for sale were legitimate or that they came from where the sellers said they did. That's true of any transaction—online or in the real world—but it was especially true when the internet was a relatively new marketplace. There weren't a lot of protections in place, and it was easier to conceal your identity. You never really knew what you were getting into.

I never had to worry about any of that with Billy. He had all these incredible pieces that nobody else could get. He knew all the artists and antiquarians living in the Lower East Side back before it was gentrified. Billy's Antiques was a throwback to a different time that was quickly disappearing.

I loved hanging out at Billy's Antiques because I never knew what I was going to find at his store. He had the craziest stuff, from high-brow to low. Billy had all kinds of antique furniture that you might expect to find at an estate sale in a wealthy enclave in New England, but he also had art pieces by Keith Haring and Joe Coleman. You'd look at a shelf full of rare books and find an antique skull mixed in with the books. It was almost like a pawn shop. He had a little of this, a little of that, but he definitely focused on the odd. Even his sign was unusual; it featured a real skull from a longhorn steer.

One time I walked into Billy's, and he asked me if there was anything in particular I was looking for.

"I'm looking for an antique skeleton," I said, certain there was no way he had one. I had, in fact, been looking for such a specimen for a long time.

Billy simply pointed with his cane, and there, of course, was a skeleton, which I bought after negotiating a lengthy payment plan.

You really could find anything at Billy's Antiques.

I was fascinated with shrunken heads long before I made my first purchase. I went to every museum I could find to learn everything I could about them. At the time, the Metropolitan Museum of Art had a few, but I don't think they're on display anymore—if they still have them at all. Ripley's Believe It or Not! boasts that it has the largest collection of shrunken heads in the United States, and I don't doubt it. I would go there to study them and learn all I could because there was a ton of misinformation about these artifacts.

For example, tiki culture embraced the image of the shrunken head, and so these artifacts became associated with South Pacific tribes that purportedly engaged in cannibalism, but the practice of shrinking heads actually originated in the Upper Amazon Basin of South America in the region now occupied by eastern Ecuador and northwestern Peru. I discovered a book called *Shrunken Heads* by Dr. James L. Castner, an entomologist who developed an interest in the subject. Castner's book became a bible for collectors because it didn't stop at the origins of the practice but documented how they became a popular source of fascination for the general public.

Billy knew about my obsession with shrunken heads, and he let me know he had one for sale. At $4,000, it was relatively expensive considering my financial situation at the time. I wanted to buy it, but I wasn't sure if the piece was authentic. The head had a little bit of deterioration that made me think it might be a replica.

One of the ways that you can tell a genuine shrunken head from a fake one is the detail of the ear, because the ear is very difficult to simulate. There's an incredible amount of detail in a human ear. When you shrink the head, that detail becomes smaller and harder to see but is still present. So I paid close attention to the ear.

The specimen Billy was trying to sell me was difficult to assess. It was wearing a little feather headdress and was incredibly small, and I thought it might be a taxidermied monkey head.

Once I determined it wasn't an animal, I did a careful study of the facial hair. I knew to look for things like ear hair, nose hair, and the eyebrows. Human facial hair grows outward from an invisible line down the center of the face. The hair on one eyebrow goes in one direction, and the hair on the other grows in the opposite direction. One way to spot a fake is if all the hair is growing in the same direction. I'd seen good fakes, but real is real, which means there will be imperfections. If a piece lacks detail and is too clean or generic-looking, it's probably a fake.

I could tell there were places that had been touched up, but in the end, after carefully studying the piece, I determined it was a legitimate shrunken head. I'd never possessed one before, and I really wanted it. I had to sell off part of my collection to buy it, but I did. I had been searching for so long, and now I finally had one.

After buying the piece from Billy, I became even more obsessed with shrunken heads—where they came from, how they came to be, the process by which they were made.

There are basically two types of shrunken heads: a tribal shrunken head (or *tsantsa*), which is a ceremonial piece used by the Shuar and other related tribes of the Upper Amazon Basin, and a tourist shrunken head, which was made using human cadavers by people without tribal affiliation for the tourist market. Tsantsas are authentic and rare; tourist heads are neither.

The tsantsas were made from heads that had been taken during battle. These shrunken heads were much more than the spoils of war; they were receptacles for the life force of vanquished enemies. The Shuar believed that the life force of a living being, something roughly analogous to the Western concept of the soul, resided in the head. When you took the head of an enemy in battle, you increased your own power. However, there were specific protocols for how the head had to be treated to prevent that energy from escaping; otherwise, you might meet your enemy again in the afterlife. Any deviation from these long-standing processes could result in bad luck or negative energy for the person who took the head. Westerners tended to think of these practices as barbaric, but it was actually a fairly elaborate moral code in which killing had immediate consequences for the killer, his family, and the entire community.

A genuine long-haired tsantsa shrunken head from the Shuar tribe of Ecuador

One of the greatest myths about shrunken heads is that there is some magical process that shrinks the entire head—skull and all—to the size of a baseball. Obviously, that's not the case. What we think of as a shrunken head is actually the skin covering the face and cranium. The process of removing the skin from the skull is very similar to procedures used for skinning animals. Then it's a matter of shrinking and curing the skin. The famed tribal arts collector Billy Jamieson told me, "It's like taking a piece of wet leather and putting it in a clothes dryer."

For the Shuar, it wasn't quite that simple. First they would take the dismembered head and simmer it in a ceramic pot of river water. They had to make sure the fire didn't get too hot, or the head would cook and that would break down the fat and burn off the hair. Sometimes I'll see a shrunken head with most of the hair gone, which is almost always the result of letting the water in the pot get too hot.

After the head had simmered for a period of time, they removed the skin. The secret is to cut from the crown of the skull to the back of the neck along the spine. In taxidermy, when you take the skin off an animal, you have to be very careful that you take just the skin and not the muscle and bone. It's the same with a shrunken head. You also want to avoid cutting or ripping the skin; it's best to keep everything in one piece. It required some skill to remove the skin from the face, and this was typically a two-person job.

Once the skin was off, they'd toss the skull into the river. The clay pot was also destroyed so that it could never be used again. Next they'd turn the skin inside out to sew the eyelids shut and scrape off any remaining flesh. Since the Shuar believed the enemy's life force escaped through the mouth, the lips were typically already sealed with sharpened sticks. Then they would reverse the skin again and sew up the cut at the back of the head. The result was a sack of skin that resembled a mask.

The Shuar would then take hot stones from the fire and put them inside the head and sew it up. This would heat up the skin to keep it pliable but also ensure that the head retained its features. As the skin reduced, they'd remove some of the stones and replace them with hot sand. After they repeated this process numerous times, the skin was rubbed with charcoal ash and smoked over a fire, which produced the dark, discolored appearance that most shrunken heads have. The whole process took several days. It couldn't be rushed.

When the head was finally ready, the Shuar would remove the sticks and sew the lips shut with twine. Then they'd put the adornments on the head. These might include colorful feathers, decorative beads, and the green iridescent wing covers of jungle beetles. The head was now approximately the size of an adult fist and ready for a series of lengthy ceremonies to ensure protection from the enemy's spirit.

Shrunken heads were known to exist as early as the sixteenth century, but as more explorers and anthropologists made their way to the Amazon Basin, interest in the phenomenon surged. The few specimens that made it out of the region were highly coveted and considered a prize item for collectors. The Shuar were fairly pragmatic people and would often trade shrunken heads for weapons and other essentials. Guns were hard to come by, but they could always procure another head.

The demand for shrunken heads was so great that, by the late nineteenth century, entrepreneurs were taking cadaver heads and shrinking them for the purpose of selling them to Europeans and Americans who would bring them home and add them to their cabinets of curiosities. Interest in shrunken heads peaked in the early twentieth century when Robert L. Ripley, founder of Ripley's Believe It or Not!, put them on display in his Odditoriums across the country and around the world. As Ripley's and places like it declined in popularity, interest waned and specimens became scarce. As of this writing, Ripley's displays at least one shrunken head at each of its Odditoriums.

———— ◆ ————

THE PROFESSOR'S COLLECTION
Ryan

Sometime after I purchased my first shrunken head at Billy's, I became aware of a large collection of heads and other oddities that belonged to a famed anthropologist who had recently passed away. This is often how it goes for me. Once I become obsessed with something, I start finding it everywhere. I suppose it's only natural that once you immerse yourself in a subculture and start learning about it, that world gradually reveals more of itself to you.

I was doing tons of research and talking to experts from around the country. As it became my main focus, people would offer to sell me pieces from their collections, refer me to other collectors, or let me know when entire collections were becoming available. That's how I found out about an astonishing collection of shrunken heads and other tribal artifacts owned by a well-known professor of anthropology in Pennsylvania who had traveled extensively during his career. Through his travels, he amassed a sizable collection of oddities. A tribal arts dealer I knew reached out to me via email. He told me about the professor's collection and that he had recently passed away. He attached a few photographs and informed me the professor's widow was trying to figure out what to do with the collection. Was I interested?

When I looked at the photos, I was blown away. While most of the pieces were obviously created for the tourist trade, they were of very high quality. There was a range, but I could tell that the collection included incredibly good specimens of shrunken heads, many of which had long hair. If you look at old photos of tribal members, their hair isn't that long, but when the scalp shrinks, the hair appears much longer. Long-haired shrunken heads tend to be more desirable and hence more valuable for aesthetic reasons. It looked as if there was at least one authentic tsantsa, though it was hard to tell from a JPEG.

I started to do some detective work. One of the photos had the professor's name on it, and from there I was able to find the email address for his widow. I sent her a message, and when she replied, we set up a call. As I continued my research, I found several blogs that were dedicated to the buying, selling, and trading of shrunken heads. As I combed over these blogs, the professor's name came up over and over again, and I could see the conversations he was having with several people in this community.

When the professor's widow sent me additional photos of his collection, I realized he was a serious collector who knew what he was doing. He had over fifty pieces, which included shrunken heads and other tribal artifacts predominantly from South America. It was without question the finest collection of oddities I'd ever come across at that point in my career.

Naturally, I started to freak out. *I have to have this collection*, I thought.

The professor's widow, however, didn't want to sell it to me. She told me she wanted to break up the collection and sell the individual pieces to auction houses or private collectors.

I couldn't let that happen. I didn't want to buy one or two things. I wanted *everything*. That has always been my mentality: Buy the entire collection because you're taking everything off their hands at once. Every collector knows what the best pieces in their collection are, but they also have things they're unsure about because there's always a chance that no one will want them. When you sell an entire collection, you're getting something for objects that might only be valuable to you.

This situation was different because it was an outstanding collection from top to bottom, and the professor's widow knew it. She was hesitant to meet with me because she wasn't interested in selling the collection as a whole.

I offered to create an auction catalog for her to better assess each of the pieces. This way she'd have a price breakdown of every item in the collection. I told her this was my specialty and by providing her with estimates for each item, she could use the catalog as a starting point when she negotiated with auction houses and private collectors.

She agreed to this, and I got to work. I took the photos she sent me and conducted extensive research on each item. After a week

Ryan working in his home studio

of very little sleep, and with some help from a graphic designer, I produced a physical catalog of the entire collection.

I called up the professor's widow and told her the catalog was ready.

"I'd like to show you my findings and discuss what you'd like to do with the collection," I said.

"Okay," she replied cautiously, "but don't get your hopes up. I'm not selling the collection to you, but you're more than welcome to come and look at it."

I agreed, but if I was going to go all the way to Pennsylvania, I wasn't coming home empty-handed.

The middle of Pennsylvania is a long way from Brooklyn, and my younger brother, Evan, offered to drive me because I didn't have a car at the time. It took us five hours to drive to where the professor had lived with his wife in a modest little house in the middle of nowhere.

Collectors are governed by emotional impulses. There's no logic behind why we like what we like or why we care about the objects in our collections as much as we do. As much as I like to believe that I'm rational and logical about my approach to buying and selling, deep down I know I'm no different from other collectors. I'm extremely superstitious, and some of my superstitions are very silly. So I'm just going to put this out there: If I hear a song by Huey Lewis and the News on the radio before making a deal, I know it's going to go well. I know that sounds kind of random, but after many deals I've found it to be absolutely, 100 percent true.

As Evan and I were going through Manhattan, "Hip to Be Square" came on the radio. We stopped mid-conversation and looked at each other.

"Holy shit," I said. "Today is going to be a good day."

I wasn't just banking on superstition. I had a briefcase full of cash in case I was able to convince the professor's widow to sell me the collection. I'd taken all the money I had out of the bank and even sold a few things from my collection to raise cash. I took all that money and put it in my leather briefcase.

This used to be my thing. When I was going to make a deal, I carried the money in my briefcase like a gangster in an old crime movie. I liked having the cash on hand because it was very cinematic. It's much more persuasive to show up with tens of thousands of dollars in cash than a checkbook. The Huey Lewis and the News song was just the icing on the cake.

When we finally showed up at the professor's house in the countryside, a man I didn't know opened the door and invited us in. He was extremely happy to see us and struck me as unusually welcoming. This was not the reception I had been expecting.

It quickly became apparent that this man was romantically involved with the professor's widow. I can imagine that for him, the collection probably felt like a lingering reminder of her late husband. It's possible he believed his partner was attached to these objects because she was still attached to the professor. The widow made it clear to me over the phone that she wasn't ready to part with the collection, but her partner had a totally different mindset. He wanted this stuff out of the house.

Over the years, I've learned that with every deal there will be people who work with you, and people who work against you. This gentleman was working with me, but he also helped me realize that although the professor's widow may have found a new partner, she hadn't completely turned the page on her past. She was still grieving.

In these situations, you need to be quick-witted and sharp, but you also have to be empathetic. You have to be able to handle many different emotions, but you can never lose sight of the fact that you're dealing with a person who has deep feelings that they may not have fully explored. You almost have to be like a therapist. Bottom line, you have to be respectful.

So instead of coming on strong, I sat with the widow and talked about her husband and learned what kind of person he was, how he was adored by his students and respected by his peers. The widow provided a fuller picture of the man so that I understood he was much more than a collector of oddities.

After we'd talked for a while, she said, "Would you like to see the collection?"

This was the moment I'd been waiting for.

The professor's widow took me into the living room, where she had all the pieces laid out, and my jaw almost hit the floor. What I thought was a collection of fifty pieces was actually twice the size. I tried my best to keep my composure while I mentally calculated the value of everything I was seeing. Again, I didn't want to jump into the deal. I wanted the professor's widow to get comfortable with me while she told me stories about how her husband had acquired some of the pieces. When she was done, I gave her the catalog I'd so painstakingly created.

She didn't even look at it.

"Let's address the elephant in the room," I ventured. "I want to buy the entire collection. This is what I think it's worth."

I threw out a number.

"No." She didn't even think about it.

Oh shit, I thought. *She really isn't ready.* I felt my heart sink because I could feel the deal slipping away. I actually became physically crippled for a moment before regaining my composure.

"If there are some items you're especially attached to," I said, "you can take them out, but I want to take everything else off your hands."

Then I raised my price.

She again said no.

I reminded her that auction houses charge hefty fees for every item they sell. So even when buyers get into a bidding war, you can still end up with less than the value of the piece after the auction house takes its cut.

Again, her answer was no.

I couldn't give up because I absolutely had to have this collection. I started with a low number, then a medium number, and then a high number. I raised my price three times. Before I made my final offer, I told the widow I had the money with me and was prepared to take the collection off her hands and pay her in cash right now.

Then I opened the briefcase.

She didn't budge.

Well, that's it, I thought. *This isn't about the money.* Other forces were holding her back. She was too emotionally invested in the collection, and she wasn't going to part with it at any price. I wasn't the only one who reached this conclusion, and much to my surprise her partner intervened.

"Please take the offer," he said to the widow. "This is a good deal. Let's get this stuff out of our lives."

The widow's partner was very keen on getting rid of the collection. I don't think he was interested in the money. I think he realized she was holding on to the collection because it was a connection to the life she'd lived with her husband, and no amount of money was going to change that. The collection was becoming increasingly uncomfortable for this new person in her life. He chose that moment to speak up and say what was on his mind, and I'm glad he did because I believe that's what pushed the widow over the edge.

Every collector has a fear of missing their chance to sell their collection to the right person for the right price. If you miss the perfect opportunity, it might never happen again. If you wait, the items could be damaged in an extreme weather event like a fire, flood, or tornado. They can degrade over time because they're not in the right environment. Anything can happen. You don't want to hold on to something too long, especially when you're not in a position to take care of it properly. At that point, a collection that was once the source of so much passion and joy becomes a burden.

The widow wasn't there yet, but it had crossed her mind. She knew that the longer this stuff sat in boxes in her living room, the greater the possibility that something might happen to it that would cause its value to go down. That's the scenario that gives every collector nightmares.

Ultimately, I think the professor's widow wanted what everybody wants: a fair price and for the collection to go to a good home, but when the time came, she was reluctant to pull the trigger—not because of her sentimental attachment to the pieces themselves but because of what they represented. When her partner pleaded his case, she realized it was time to let them go.

That's when she finally agreed.

I paid her the money—just about all the money I had in the briefcase, which was all the money I had in the world—and packed up the professor's collection. His widow's partner helped me carry the pieces out to the car. Maybe he was afraid the widow would change her mind. We said our goodbyes and drove away.

After we had driven a few blocks, I told my brother to pull over. I opened the door and threw up in the gutter. I'd spent so much energy trying to keep my composure and remain calm that when the deal was done, I felt completely overwhelmed. I was full of adrenaline during the sale. When I threw up, all that nervous energy literally poured out of me.

I'd bought my first major collection, which was huge, but now I was completely broke. I'd spent nearly every penny I had to purchase a bunch of shrunken heads. Was I crazy?

I was practically in shock, a shell of myself, and I remained so until we returned to Brooklyn and I started to go through the professor's massive collection the next day.

It was such a big haul that it took me a long time to go through it all, and along the way I made some shocking discoveries. Because the professor traveled to South America pretty frequently, I assumed he'd picked up most of the pieces during his travels. While it's true that many of the skulls in his collection originated in South America, it turned out that several of them were acquired through New York auction houses many years ago.

This meant I was able to determine the provenance of many of the items in the collection, which is very important when you're dealing with human remains. I was now able to pinpoint exactly where these pieces had come from, how they had entered the country, and when. In the past, collectors weren't always concerned with the provenance of the pieces they bought and sold, but times have changed. Many museums with natural history collections are discovering that they don't have documentation for how they came to own certain items. That's a problem—both legally and ethically.

There are very strict rules about buying, selling, and transporting archaeological artifacts. You need to know those rules, and you need to be aware of the laws. For instance, in the United States, skulls can't be imported to certain states, and they can't be imported to or exported from certain countries. Knowing the history of the items in your collection is essential. Even today, there are dealers who aren't concerned with provenance. They just want the goods and don't care about where they came from. I'm not one of them.

Going through a collection is a time-consuming process because you have to document everything, and you don't want the pieces to get mixed up. If I don't have all of the documentation for a piece, the way it's packaged can provide a clue. For example, the skulls and shrunken heads in this collection were stuffed with antique newspapers from Ecuador. This helps the shrunken heads retain their shape and provides some extra padding during shipping, but the fact that the newspapers were Ecuadorian and that each page was stamped with the date helped with the authentication process.

I'm notoriously slow when it comes to going through a new collection. I can spend months and months in my studio going through the items before I decide what to do with them. As much as I want to spend time with all of the new pieces so that I completely understand what I have, I still have a life to live and a business to run. I never want to rush the process. In addition to documenting each piece, I'm also preparing it for display. My mantra has always been to treat each piece with the utmost respect. That means cleaning it, restoring it, making a stand for it, and presenting it like it's the best artifact in my collection.

While it's fairly typical to find shrunken heads stuffed with newspaper, it's unusual to find newspapers inside of skulls. That was the case with some of these skulls, and at first I was hesitant to remove them. Maybe there was a reason why they were in there. I wanted to be careful, so I left the newspapers inside the skulls until I had time to go through them.

Several months after I bought the collection, I made a startling discovery. I was working on one of the skulls in my studio and carefully removing the newspaper stuffed inside when I realized there was something else wedged in there, crammed inside the skull.

What the heck is this? I wondered.

Whatever it was had been wrapped so tightly that I found it difficult to get it out. I carefully removed all the newspapers so that I could extract this little bundle, which was also wrapped in newspaper. I slowly unwrapped the Ecuadorian newspaper and found a necklace inside—a necklace made of human fingers.

It was an incredibly rare artifact. I had only seen two finger necklaces previously. One was at the Smithsonian, and the other belonged to the famed collector Billy Jamieson, so I brought the necklace to him to see what he could tell me about it.

Jamieson was a high-end collector of tribal arts based in Toronto, and I really admired him. He had a TV show called *Treasure Trader* on the History Channel. He was famous for buying the collection of the Niagara Falls Museum. The natural history museum had fallen on hard times, and rather than sell off pieces one by one to keep the place running, they decided to liquidate the entire collection. Jamieson swooped in and bought the whole museum—all seven hundred thousand pieces. It must have cost him millions of dollars, but he made it all back with one incredible discovery.

The Niagara Falls Museum was an extensive Victorian affair with all kinds of animal skeletons and dinosaur bones, which can go for huge sums. The museum also had an assortment of mummies, one of which turned out to be Pharaoh Ramses I, founder of ancient Egypt's nineteenth dynasty, which the museum didn't know it had in its possession. Jamieson sold the mummy to another museum, and that sale essentially paid for the whole collection. (Ramses I has since been repatriated to Egypt.)

Jamieson knew quite a bit about the origins of the finger necklace. He told me that in Papua New Guinea, the Kukukuku tribe had a practice of making necklaces from plant matter, feathers, and finger bones. These weren't war trophies. When an ancestor died, the family would take one of the deceased's fingers, preserve it, and make it into

a necklace as a form of memento mori, a sign of remembrance of the dead. With the passing of each elder, another finger was added to the necklace, so that over time the necklace served as a kind of family tree. While this may seem like a grisly practice to us, this tradition was an important aspect of mourning and cultural memory for members of the tribe.

Regina modeling a genuine finger neck-lace from the Angu or Änga people, also called Kukukuku

After acquiring the professor's collection, I became the go-to guy for shrunken heads in the city. I sold four of the heads in the collection and recouped my original investment. That left me with six shrunken heads plus all the other pieces. You would think that would satisfy my curiosity, but the more I learned about the new additions to my collection, the more I wanted.

That's the thing when you're a collector: If you get one, you want another one. If you get ten, you want ten more. Suddenly, you're devoting all your time and energy on this one thing. The more information you seek, the more interesting it becomes. Collecting is like becoming immersed in a very intense relationship. It doesn't matter if you're collecting rare baseball cards or shrunken heads. It's the same feeling. It's almost like an obsession.

Acquiring the professor's collection led me to learn more about the marketplace and the other players in it. At that time, there weren't a ton of people collecting these kinds of objects because they were so rare and expensive. They're even more expensive now because there are more collectors and fewer available artifacts. They don't become available nearly as often as they used to.

In the end, the finger necklace ended up being the rarest specimen in the professor's collection. It's possible the professor wasn't aware of what he had, but there's no way of knowing. I no longer have any of those shrunken heads in my collection. The market has changed, and so have my interests. My collection has evolved to reflect my passion for artwork crafted by human hands.

I have fond memories of those pieces because they formed the first important collection I purchased, but it certainly wasn't the last.

———— ◆•◆ ————

STOLEN OR NOT?
Ryan & Regina

We typically don't deal in shrunken heads anymore. Our interests are always evolving from one thing to the next. What we're obsessed with today may seem passé tomorrow. Most authentic shrunken heads have found their way to a handful of high-end collectors and museums, some of which have been quietly repatriating them back to Ecuador according to guidelines outlined by that country's National Institute of Cultural Heritage (INPC). As society's attitudes about exhibiting human remains have changed over the years, some cultural institutions and universities have taken steps to return these specimens to their countries of origin. Once a piece has been authenticated, however, it's up to the discretion of entities like Ecuador's INPC to determine if they want the artifact back, which isn't always the case.

In early 2016, we purchased a pair of shrunken heads from a high-end gallery and auction house in New York City. We have done a lot of business with this gallery and over the years have spent well over six figures with them. Some of the items we sold to other collectors, and some pieces were for our own collection. This particular auction house has been in business since 1961 and is a reputable source for ethnographic items.

Whenever this gallery obtained a shrunken head or a rare oddity, they would contact us because we had done so much business together and it wasn't really their specialty.

When the gallery offered us the pair of shrunken heads, we replied, "We'll take them." We purchased the pieces because we knew we would be able to find clients for them. One piece was subpar, but the other was a very good specimen. We posted photos on social media and were able to sell the artifacts fairly quickly to two different private collectors for a very good profit.

A few weeks later, we got a call from the head curator at Ripley's Believe It or Not! in Times Square.

"What's up?" I asked, happy to hear from him.

"I wanted to let you know that two shrunken heads were stolen from our collection, and we think you may have them."

"Holy shit!" I said. "Send us some pictures."

The curator emailed photos of the missing pieces, and sure enough they were the two shrunken heads that we'd just sold.

We now had a dilemma on our hands. There was no question that we would try to get the heads back for Ripley's, but we'd sold these pieces for quite a lot of money. The collectors weren't going to be happy to discover they'd purchased stolen goods.

We called each of the collectors and told them the bad news: "We're really sorry, but we need the head back."

One of the collectors understood the situation, but the other was pretty upset. The only way he would return the head was if we exchanged it for one from our private collection. We agreed because we didn't want to lose him as a customer. Also, it was imperative that we get the stolen merchandise back for Ripley's because it had been a big story in the news. Apparently, the thieves had also stolen some baseball memorabilia—a rare 1941 Joe DiMaggio bat and some baseballs autographed by DiMaggio and Ted Williams.

The thieves were clearly amateurs because the baseball items themselves weren't worth that much without the certificates of authenticity. But why had they also stolen a pair of shrunken heads?

It was a mystery.

Next, we contacted the gallery that sold us the heads.

"First off, you sold us stolen goods," we said to our contact. "Second, we'll bring the stolen shrunken heads back, but you need to return them to Ripley's and give us a full refund!"

Our gallery contact was stunned. He said someone had walked into the gallery without an appointment with a story about how the shrunken heads belonged to his grandfather. He said the guy found them in his grandfather's trunk in the attic and brought them to the gallery to see if they were worth anything. The story wasn't that outlandish. People were always finding unusual items their parents or grandparents had stashed away, from World War II memorabilia to old newspaper clippings. Shrunken heads were a rare example, although not unheard of.

Ultimately, everything ended well. Ripley's got their shrunken heads, and almost everyone got their money back. Unfortunately, stories like this are not uncommon. Even reputable galleries with impeccable reputations can get duped into thinking they're buying legitimate goods.

The point is that you never really know what you're buying. You have to trust what the seller is telling you, which is why the provenance is so important.

Not too long ago Nicolas Cage and Leonardo DiCaprio got into a bidding war at an auction over a dinosaur skull. Cage won the battle but lost the war when he found out that the *Tyrannosaurus bataar* skull he'd paid over a quarter of a million dollars for was stolen and had to be returned to Mongolia.

Kim Kardashian reportedly purchased an ancient Italian statue from an art dealer only to find out that it had been illegally exported and in all likelihood had been looted.

More recently, an art gallery in Miami came under fire for holding an exhibit of newly discovered Jean-Michel Basquiat paintings. There was a ton of publicity, and all kinds of celebrities turned out for the opening. Unfortunately, the paintings were all completely fake.

These deceptions took place at high-end galleries and prestigious auction houses. In cases like these, it's not the buyer's fault they were lied to. It's the responsibility of the seller to ensure the authenticity of a sale.

What's interesting is that a lot of collectors don't care if an object is fake. As long as it's interesting and cool, they're okay with it.

Not us. We treat everything as if it's an investment. If we're buying something, we have to know that everything is correct because some day we may want to sell that piece, and then the responsibility will fall to us to ensure its authenticity.

Not too long ago, someone sent us a photo of a shrunken head.

"Check out this amazing shrunken head I just bought."

"How much did you pay for it?" I asked.

"Ten grand."

"Hate to tell you this, but that is a monkey head."

The seller had conned this individual into thinking they'd bought an authentic shrunken head, but we were able to tell it was a fake just by looking at the photograph.

To protect our customers and our reputation, we have to make sure that everything is on the up-and-up. We have to be very, very careful because even the most knowledgeable person on earth can still get had. On the handful of occasions that we've been sold a false bill of goods, we've been able to avoid legal repercussions because we always do the right thing.

We've bought paintings that turned out to be forgeries. Sometimes we were able to get a refund from the seller. Other times we couldn't. It just goes to show that no one is immune from falling for a good story. There's no feeling more powerful than wanting something to be true.

CHAPTER IV

CABINETS

OF

CURIOSITIES

A Cabinet of My Own

From Obscura to *Oddities*

After *Oddities*

Ryan and Regina during their first trip together to Paris. One of their favorite museums is the Galerie de Paléontologie et d'Anatomie comparée.

A CABINET OF MY OWN
Ryan

I 've always wanted to live in a museum.

Ever since I was a kid, I've been obsessed with museums. I loved walking through the various halls, looking at the artifacts arranged in elaborate cabinets and the natural specimens displayed in realistic-looking dioramas. When I went to a museum, I felt transported back in time, and I never wanted to leave. I used to think, "How cool would it be to live here?" It was something I muttered frequently throughout my childhood. Museums were magical places.

It wasn't just the objects themselves that I found captivating. I've always been fascinated by how they were presented in such an engaging manner. When I first started collecting, I was extremely interested in displaying my own collection in a way that was aesthetically appealing—just like a museum. How could I faithfully recreate that aesthetic?

As I progressed deeper into collecting, I started looking into the history of museums. I needed to know why their artifacts were selected, who collected them, and how they showed them off.

The urge to collect has existed for many centuries. The origins of the modern museum can be found in the reliquaries of medieval churches and cathedrals. These places of worship displayed holy relics: a vial of a saint's blood or the bones of a holy figure. Because there was a great deal of interest in these objects, no expense was spared in putting them on display so they could be admired and venerated by worshippers. Reliquaries were often made of brass, silver, or gold and were usually much more elegant-looking than the objects they contained.

Worshippers making a pilgrimage from one place to another might stop at a church along the way just to see its collection of holy treasures, many of which stretched the limits of credulity. From the head of Saint John the Baptist to the arm of Saint George the Dragon Slayer to "the Holy Prepuce" (i.e., the foreskin of baby Jesus), these objects attracted large crowds. The goal of reliquaries was to inspire a sense of wonder in the viewer. The relics provided proof of God's presence through the extraordinary faith of these saints and martyrs.

Were the relics authentic? Probably not, but the wonder that onlookers felt in their presence was real.

As the Dark Ages drew to a close and Europe inched toward the Enlightenment, a spirit of scientific discovery seized the educated and the elite. Explorers, naturalists, and soldiers brought back all kinds of unusual artifacts from their journeys to far-off lands. Men of science, culture, and means began to collect and display taxidermied creatures, ethnographic oddities, rare specimens from the natural world, and unusual works of art.

Though the contents were different, the goal of these displays was similar to that of reliquaries: to instill wonder in those who looked upon these extraordinary objects. In Germany, collectors called the rooms where these collections were held *Kunstkammer* (cabinets of curiosities) or *Wunderkammer* (chambers of wonder). Some of the specimens in these cabinets were collected for educational purposes, while others served as keepsakes from their owners' adventures in distant lands. Where a relic of a sainted figure stood in for the whole person, a well-stocked cabinet symbolized humankind's quest for knowledge and dominion over the natural world.

As these cabinets become more popular, the urge to possess the biggest, the rarest, and the most wondrous specimens led to larger collections that could no longer be contained in a single room. The origins of museums can be traced back to this urge to share the wonders of the world and inspire the curiosity of all who looked upon them. Who knew such things existed? Who knew such wonders were possible?

That's how it was for me. I longed to have a cabinet of curiosities of my own, but my life was anything but stable. I lived in insufficient apartments all over New York and had all kinds of hustles and many major setbacks in my younger

Various European reliquary hands that once held the relics of deceased saints

years. My first apartment was in Boerum Hill, Brooklyn, but I didn't stay there long as it was only a six-month sublet. Then I moved to Bushwick, which was horrible because my apartment was incredibly small and not in the greatest neighborhood. I was there for only about a year, and then I moved to a more expensive apartment in Fort Greene.

During this time, I moved to Rome for a few months, which ended up being a total disaster. I didn't have a lot of money, and living in Italy was very expensive. The most affordable place to dine was a

Chinese restaurant close to where I was staying. I ate Chinese food almost every night and missed out on a lot of the legendary Italian cuisine.

When I got back to Fort Greene, I found out I was being evicted. Before I left for Rome, I had sublet my apartment to someone I had met on Craigslist, which was how you found a subletter in the city back in the day. While I was away in Rome, my subletter never bothered to pay the rent, and the landlord didn't tell me. Upon my return to New York, I found I owed the landlord $10,000 in back rent and fees. I didn't have that kind of money, so the landlord told me to get the fuck out, and I did. I removed some of my stuff that day, and when I came back to get the rest of my belongings, there was a padlock on the door. The guy locked me out of my own apartment.

I had nowhere to live and no way to get my stuff back. I did everything I could to get a hold of the landlord—it was the early 2000s, and I still didn't have a cell phone—but the guy wouldn't return my calls. He just took all my stuff. Furniture, all of my art, sketchbooks, antiques, you name it. My most prized possession at the time was a vintage 1920s glass-topped embalming table that you could raise or lower with an industrial crank. It was absolutely incredible, and I've never seen another one quite like it. They are impossible to find and now it was gone.

The majority of my collection was safe, but just about everything else I had in that apartment was taken from me. I lost all of my art. I still get sick to my stomach thinking about it. Ten years later, this same landlord sued me for the back rent plus interest, and I had to settle with him for a large sum of money.

After Fort Greene, I moved to Park Slope for a while. At this point, I was moving every six months to a year, and the places kept getting smaller and the rents kept getting larger. It wasn't just me.

It seemed like everyone I knew in New York was constantly on the move. I found myself in a pattern of moving to get out of a bad situation only to end up in one that was even worse.

From Park Slope I moved to St. Mark's Place in Manhattan, right on the main drag above an old shop called Freaks. I lived in a closet. That's not a metaphor. I lived in an actual closet that I turned into my living quarters.

Needless to say, I didn't have a lot of space during this period when I was roaming around, so I wasn't adding much to my collection. I didn't want to buy a bunch of stuff because I knew I'd be on the move again soon. I was looking for things that I could flip quickly. Being so close to the flea markets was a huge advantage. I would get interested in something, become completely obsessed with it, and use that obsession to make money to live.

I looked for anything vintage, especially things that could be bought and sold easily, like vintage concert T-shirts. For a brief moment in the early 2000s, T-shirts that you could have found in literally any Salvation Army a few years before were going for hundreds of dollars in the boutique thrift stores that were popping up all over the place. I focused on early rock bands, heavy metal, and humorous shirts. This provided enough income to pay my rent, which was only $400 at the time.

When I was living on St. Mark's, I got really obsessed with collecting rare muscle bikes, which are kid's bicycles from the '60s with banana seats, sissy bars, and high handlebars. They were designed to emulate the chopper motorcycles that were popular with bikers. I found early Raleigh Choppers and Schwinn Sting-Rays all over the city and sold them to my friends or to other collectors in the area. I even bought a bicycle designed by the famed artist George Barris, who created custom cars for Hollywood, including the Batmobile, Eddie Munster's chain bicycle, and Elvira's 1959 Ford Thunderbird convertible, which appeared on her TV show. He also did a lot of pinstripe work and custom modifications on classic cars.

I'd find rare bikes at flea markets or on Craigslist, fix them up, and sell them to collectors. I ended up selling several of my bicycles to a muscle bike museum in New England that is now defunct. I was literally wheeling and dealing with anything that would turn a profit. It just goes to show that if something is rare, interesting, or unique, there's a community of people who find it valuable.

I left the closet on St. Mark's because I had planned on moving to Los Angeles but somehow ended up in San Diego. It's actually a funny story. I was supposed to go to Los Angeles with a woman I was dating. I moved all my stuff into my mom's house in upstate New York, and right before we were getting ready to leave for the West Coast, my girlfriend dumped me.

A friend who was driving out to California to go into drug rehab came to the rescue.

"Yo, I'm driving to LA if you want to ride with me," she said.

"Fuck it. Let's go!"

I'd already moved out of the city and figured I might as well go since moving in with my mother wasn't really an option. I had a friend in San Diego who said I could stay with him until I figured things out. I loaded all of my meager possessions in a little Honda Civic, and we drove across the country. She dropped me off in San Diego, waved goodbye, and headed off to rehab.

I had brought a couple of suitcases and my guitar. I didn't even have a case for the guitar. I'd brought a low-rider bicycle with me for cheap and easy transportation. My friend greeted me at the door, and I could see right away that the place was a shithole. He was a tattoo artist and a major pot smoker and didn't really have his life together.

"Where's my room?" I asked.

"Here," my friend said, giving me a deflated air mattress. It turned out that it wasn't his place at all. It belonged to a friend of his. He and I shared the living room together, sleeping on the filthy floor, and I had no privacy. I remember one night I was so fed up with my friend that I ended up sleeping in a tent on a skateboard ramp in the backyard. I lasted about a week before a couple I met offered me their extra room and let me stay at their place for a while.

I ended up meeting another guy through a Craigslist ad who wanted to start a rock band, and that finally got me up to LA. We got the band going and made a go of it, but the band sucked. I repeated this process with two or three other bands—all of which were unsuccessful. I only lasted a few months in LA before I went back to New York. LA was like a fever dream. I just couldn't deal with the lifestyle. To this day, I remember very few details from my time there.

I was back in Brooklyn, but I wasn't ready to give up my rock and roll dreams. A friend of mine, Andy Animal, was looking for a rhythm guitar player for his band, Stalkers. I'd known him since I was thirteen, and we were best friends growing up in Woodstock, New York. We were basically Beavis and Butt-Head. Stalkers was a low-down dirty rock and roll band that had more in com-

Ryan (far left) during his days as a rock and roll star playing guitar with Stalkers

mon with the New York Dolls and the Dead Boys than the Strokes or the Yeah Yeah Yeahs. Stalkers had made a huge name for itself in the NYC music scene. I was constantly asking Andy to let me join the band, and he finally relented after I came back from LA.

Somehow Stalkers managed to get a record deal. We were signed to a subsidiary of Warner Brothers and even went out on tour, but the band was a mess. There was a lot of hard partying going on, and that was never my scene. I liked to drink and hang out, but I'd get so nervous before performing that I was a wreck by the time we got onstage. We were a total disaster. We would occasionally get into fistfights onstage during the show, but the music was great. Once I realized I liked the idea of being in a band more than I liked actually playing in one, I packed up my guitar.

It was a weird time, but the experience helped clarify a few things for me in terms of what I did and didn't want to do with my life.

Even though I only lived on the West Coast for six months at the most, when I got back to New York, the city felt different. When I first started going to the Lower East Side to look for material for my art projects, it was like another world. I would wander around the streets of Manhattan and find tons of little antique stores all over Chinatown and the Lower East Side that were filled with exciting things I'd never seen before.

These little stores reminded me of P & T Surplus in Kingston, New York, which I first started going to when I was a teenager. There's no way to describe the place without making it sound like I'm making it up. P & T Surplus was filled with so much strange stuff that it was hard to get a handle on who it was for other than misfits like me. There'd be bins of weird electronic parts and doll hands alongside used tools and old mannequins. I'd go in there and fill up a bag for $20. Then I'd take my loot home and use it in my art projects.

When I got back from California, I noticed that a lot of the small antique stores I'd frequented were starting to disappear. Rents were going up and corporations were moving in, putting the squeeze on small business owners. There was no way these little shops could afford to stay in business.

Just a few years earlier, I could find antiques all over the city. If I found a cool-looking oddity, I'd buy it for next to nothing. Then I'd hit every tattoo shop on the Lower East Side until I found a buyer for it. I'd just sell stuff out of a bag, or the tattooer would offer a barter. The barter system was alive and well back then, and I utilized it on many occasions. I knew a guy named Scott Campbell who eventually became a famous tattoo artist. He had a shop in Williamsburg, Brooklyn, that he shared with a friend's antique shop. I remember trading a Victorian taxidermied fox head for the swallow tattoos I have on my hands.

As eBay became more popular, many of those little mom-and-pop antique shops moved online. As the rents increased, antiquarians couldn't afford to operate their brick-and-mortar stores anymore. The younger collectors were quick to embrace emerging technology, while the older generation held on to the old ways until they were priced out of the neighborhoods where they had been in business for decades. Once they disappeared, they didn't come back. They're all gone now and with them the wonder they inspired.

I was fortunate enough to get into collecting before all the old antique stores disappeared. I was there for the wild west of collecting at the turn of the twenty-first century when the pickings were plentiful. I was living hand to mouth and wouldn't go back to those days, but I miss getting up at dawn and hitting the flea markets, never really knowing if I was going to find something extraordinary. That was part of the excitement: the hunt for something I'd never seen before.

All the moving around I'd done really put the brakes on my collecting. On the plus side, I was keeping the best pieces because I didn't have the space to accumulate a lot of other stuff. You need space to be a hoarder.

Every time I had to move, I'd pack up my collection and put all my art supplies away. Sometimes it would take months for me to unpack it all, and then it would be time to move again. It wasn't until I moved into an apartment in Greenpoint, Brooklyn, that I finally had a place that was big enough to display my collection properly and facilitate my art.

The apartment was only 1,200 square feet, but by New York City standards, that was enormous. More importantly, it had high ceilings. Once I got the right cabinetry installed, I could display my collection all the way from the floor to the ceiling, and it looked stunning. I had achieved my goal of creating a cabinet of curiosities of my own. It was finally starting to feel like I was living in a museum.

———•••———

FROM OBSCURA TO *ODDITIES*
Ryan

Obscura Antiques and Oddities became my favorite store the moment I walked into the place. Obscura was originally located on Tenth Street between First Avenue and Avenue A. Even though it was just two rooms, it was filled from floor to ceiling with the rarest skulls, skeletons, taxidermy, and medical devices. They had the most obscure antiques I had ever seen—all the stuff that I was interested in when I moved to the city. What made Obscura great, however, was the people who worked there.

Obscura was originally run by Mike Zohn, Evan Michelson, and Adrian Gilboe. Adrian actually started Obscura in the 1990s when it was called Wandering Dragon Trading Company. He had one of the best eyes in the business, but he was *very* hard to deal with. He ended up leaving—partly due to business differences but mainly because of his drinking, which ended up killing him in the end.

At Obscura, sometimes I would buy stuff, sometimes I would sell things, but mostly I went there to hang out. I clicked with the people who worked there, and I loved the atmosphere they created. It felt exactly like what I imagined the salons of nineteenth-century explorers and naturalists who created cabinets of curiosities were like. You never knew who was going to come through the door: doctors, celebrities, or weirdos like me. Obscura was a unique place, and in all the years I've been in this business, I've never seen anyone replicate it.

Ryan outside of Obscura Antiques during the filming of the TV show *Oddities*

After I'd been working at my metalcraft for a few years and designing my own line of jewelry, I was invited to go into business with Jake Mueser and Amber Doyle, friends from the music scene who were starting a bespoke suiting shop.

"Hey, I'm thinking of renting a space in a bar," Jake said one day. "Do you want to do the jewelry for it?"

"I'm in!"

We had all of our friends help us set up the shop. We opened up a little appointment-only bespoke suit and custom jewelry store in Elsa Bar on East Third Street in the East Village. People going in and out of the bar would look at our stuff, and if something caught their eye, they'd contact us.

At the time, I was making all kinds of jewelry with teeth and bone. One item that I created that became quite popular was a necklace made with a single tooth. I'd sculpt these little teardrop bezels that would go over the root of the tooth. Sometimes I'd put a little jewel in the tooth that matched the color of the buyer's birthstone. People would put them on a chain and wear them around their neck. Perhaps the tooth belonged to a parent or someone close that they wanted to remember, or they used their own baby teeth.

Ryan working in his studio at Against Nature on Chrystie Street in NYC

I was also making jewelry inspired by natural history, like medallions of lion's heads with rubies in their mouths. I sold a handful of pieces out of that location, and then we moved to a second-story shop on Chrystie Steet where Jake and all these punk rock kids were living. The shop was next to Sammy's Roumanian Steakhouse, an icon of the Lower East Side.

I did all the jewelry, Jake and Amber did all the suiting, and we had another guy named Simon Jacobs who did custom denim. That was my first real brick-and-mortar store. We called it Against Nature, after the novel of the same name by Joris-Karl Huysmans about a dandy.

We had a ton of success right off the bat. Before the store even opened, I was featured in a *New York Times* article titled "The New Antiquarians" about the younger generation of collectors. The article hyped the store's opening and was even kind enough to tell readers where to find us.

Against Nature was a hit. We stayed busy and had a lot of celebrity clients. Not only did I sell pieces that were on display in the store, but I took custom orders as well. Sometimes I'd even get special requests from stores in Japan that wanted imitations of Ralph Lauren items I had created—anything from sterling silver skulls to leather belts and bags.

"Can you make a Navajo-style bracelet?"

"I can do that," I'd say.

"Great! We'll take one hundred."

The business kept me busy. We'd been open for about a year and a half when I got a call from Mike at Obscura.

"Hey, guess what? Discovery Channel is interested in doing a show on Obscura. Would you be interested in being on the show?"

Mike explained that they needed people to fill out the cast. I would appear on the show as a buyer and private collector as well as the person in charge of restorations.

"Sure," I said, but I didn't think much of it. A show about oddities? It wasn't totally out of the realm of possibility. There were photo shoots at Obscura and Against Nature all the time, but the idea that someone would base a TV show around this strange little subculture I was so passionate about seemed a little far-fetched to me.

Sure enough, the network called and invited me in for a reading. I sat in front of a camera, and they interviewed me.

"Tell us about yourself," they asked. "What do you do?"

"Well," I said, "I make exploded skulls."

I don't know what they were expecting, but it probably wasn't that. I told them about my passion for osteological art, my jewelry business, and my large collection of oddities. I was pretty sure they thought I was a total weirdo. I didn't expect a callback.

About a week later, I heard from Mike.

"I think the show is actually going to happen," he said.

"That's great!" I said.

"Do you even have the time for this?" Mike asked. He knew how insanely busy I was. "Seriously, do you think you can devote a month to film ten episodes?"

"No, I don't," I said, "but I'm gonna make sure that I do."

My first shoot was in upstate New York. We went to an antique store and bought a taxidermy bird diorama. Before the shoot, I was very nervous, but once I got used to the cameras I felt completely comfortable. Being on camera came very naturally to me. I was able to speak intelligently about whatever I was presenting because it wasn't an act. I'd had a lot of experience buying and selling unusual artifacts, and I was genuinely passionate about it.

I was in just about every episode that first season. Although the show was mainly about the objects that people brought into the store, some of the subplots involved buying trips and preparations I'd made for the show. I demonstrated how to make an exploded skull as well as various pieces of taxidermy.

My relationship with Mike and Evan on-screen was pretty much the same as it was in real life. Mike and I did a lot of business before and during the show. He would sell me stuff that he'd found, and I'd sell him pieces from my collection. I would restore stuff for both Mike and Evan, which became part of the show. They'd ask me to make a stand for a piece that wasn't for sale but that they wanted to display in the shop. Ultimately, that's why they brought me on to the show. They needed someone who could take things that were in rough shape and make them beautiful again.

We needed guests, so we called all the interesting people we knew and asked them if they wanted to be on the show. One of the people I reached out to was none other than Andy Animal from Stalkers.

Andy came on the show, and everyone loved him. He wasn't really a collector, but he had this infectious laugh that was a cross between Butt-Head and a cackling bear, so the producers kept bringing him on. I think they wanted him to have a role like Chumlee, who is a popular character on the show *Pawn Stars*, which came out around the same time as *Oddities*. Andy would drag things into the store that he found out in the woods or down in his father's basement—like the time he brought in a giant mechanical clown. He breathed life into the show every time he came through the door.

Ryan with "Dr. Dave" filming an "OTF" (on the fly) interview for an episode of *Oddities*

We also brought in more established antiquarians, like Billy Leroy of Billy's Antiques, and other weirdo artists, collectors, and assorted freakazoids whom we knew from the neighborhood. We'd have them bring some bizarre item into the store, and they became part of the show. In my opinion, that's really what made *Oddities* stand out from other shows. Sure, it's cool to be looking at some rare or unusual object—like a skeleton foot or a taxidermied bat—but more often than not the people who brought these things into Obscura were much more interesting. I think that's what viewers really loved about *Oddities*.

The first episode aired on November 4, 2010, and the first season ran until January 20, 2011. After that, we felt there was no way the show would continue. None of us had any expectation that *Oddities* would ever amount to anything. We tried something different, and unlike other reality shows, we weren't pretending to be something we weren't. But we weren't expecting anything to come of it. We were quite content to live in cult infamy as those weirdos on TV who came and went.

When the network said they wanted to do a second season, we were all kind of baffled. In the city, hardly anyone had cable, so it was hard to gauge how many people were actually tuning in to watch our little show. Maybe more people were watching than we realized.

It definitely felt like the right people were watching because after the first season, I got so busy doing custom orders for all the people who contacted me that I ended up having to leave Against Nature. I just didn't have enough time to do it anymore. I loved making jewelry, but that was just one aspect of my passion for unusual artifacts. I was earning money with my osteological preparations and continuing to buy and sell antiques. *Oddities* seemed like a great place to showcase all the different things I could do and was interested in, so I signed on for the second season.

Oddities came along during the boom in unscripted television, and we started filming the second season almost as soon as the first season aired. My role was expanded, and I was given more screen time during the second season. I was now the resident expert in osteological endeavors. That was my specialty. If someone wanted something restored, they came to me, and a lot of the episodes focused on creating preparations for people. Also, the show started to attract more celebrities. During our second season, we had actress Chloë Sevigny on the show, and Jonathan Davis of Korn also made an appearance. The show's popularity catapulted from there.

It got to the point where elderly women would stop me in the street and say, "Hey, you're the exploded skull guy!"

I couldn't believe it. We actually had fans!

Exploded skulls became a semi-regular part of the show. I exploded a monkey skull. I exploded a human skull. I exploded skulls in various ways for a variety of people. And I articulated different types of bones in interesting ways. Thanks to *Oddities*, people now knew what an exploded skull was, and it became something that I was known for—almost like a weird trademark.

What's funny is that people watching at home thought that Mike and Evan were married. They *were* both married, but not to each other. They were just business partners who happened to love oddities. One of the secrets of the show is that Mike and Evan didn't get along that well. They would have disagreements off set, but when they were on camera together, they looked like the best of friends. It was never an issue for me because I had a great relationship with both of them. Meanwhile, I was getting a hundred emails a week with all kinds of requests for osteological preparations. Naturally, some of them were quite bizarre.

Another original osteological preparation by Ryan, in which he cut a skull horizontally for people in the medical field to study different aspects of the human cranium

"My dad was buried. If we can exhume the body, can you articulate his skeleton?"

"Sorry, we don't do that," I would say.

Another time, a fan of the show wrote to say he had to get his foot amputated. He wanted to send the foot to me so I could clean it and articulate it. I didn't take that job, but a friend of mine did, and now this poor guy's foot rests on a stand in a glass case in his living room.

Most of the emails were pretty standard requests for restoring a piece of taxidermy, with the occasional inquiry from heartbroken animal lovers who wanted to preserve their recently deceased pets. I still get email requests about that almost every week.

One of my favorite episodes involved creating an articulated skeleton for the musician Sean Lennon, son of John Lennon of the Beatles and Yoko Ono. He hired me to create a chimera, which is a mythological creature composed of various animal parts. It might have the head of a lion or the tail of a snake. Chimera Music is also the name of Sean's label and artist collective. Obviously, I'd never seen a chimera before since they don't exist in real life, so I had to use my imagination. I started with a cat skeleton as my base and replaced the feet and skull with monkey bones. Then I added bat wings to complete the illusion that this fantastical being could take flight.

I also did a project for model and musician Charlotte Kemp Muhl, who was dating Sean and wanted to buy him a shrunken head and make a cane topper out of it.

"I know it's a tall order, but is that something you could do?" she asked.

"Of course."

I took a shrunken head that I had recently purchased and filled it with epoxy that wouldn't expand, and then I embedded hardware inside the head so you could screw it onto any cane as long as the threads matched. The head had these earrings dangling from it so it looked really cool, and both Charlotte and Sean were thrilled.

Around the time that *Oddities* was at the peak of its popularity, filmmaker and author Guillermo del Toro contacted me out of the blue.

"I love your exploded skulls. Would you be interested in making one for me?"

"I'd love to," I said. I was a huge fan of his work.

I had this really nice old skull, and it was already disarticulated. It must have been used as a teaching tool for medical professionals because the bones were all numbered. I made a beautiful Beauchêne skull for him, and he displayed it on the table where he conducted his meetings. The skull I made for him was also part of his exhibition "At Home with Monsters" at the Los Angeles County Museum of Art.

Looking back, there's only one aspect of *Oddities* that I find a little embarrassing. The producers thought it would spice things up for me to have a love interest on the show. They asked me if I would go on some dates with one of the women who was a regular at Obscura. I agreed because I thought it would be good for the show, and they fixed me up with a Goth girl named Monique. There were two or three episodes that featured our "dates."

What a lot of people in the general public don't realize is that the dates weren't real. Monique and I didn't actually date in real life. When the show was at its peak in popularity, people would stop me in Target or the grocery store and ask me about Monique. They thought we were a couple, which got awkward when Regina and I were dating and strangers kept bringing up my imaginary TV show girlfriend, Monique.

All good things must come to an end, and after five seasons and seventy-five episodes, *Oddities* was canceled. We had signed a new contract for the sixth season and had even started shooting new episodes when a new CEO came in and cleaned house, killing off most of the network's original programming, including *Oddities*. It was an extremely successful show, and it's a shame that politics at the network put a stop to it. We weren't the only show they canceled. They fired almost everyone, which was the only way we could feel good about the situation.

Right before the show was canceled, the producers took the cast out to dinner at a steak house in Midtown Manhattan. The purpose of the meeting was to tell us the news, but everyone already knew what our fate was going to be, so it ended up being a bittersweet death dinner. At the table next to us sat yuppie lawyers and hedge fund bros. We noticed them pointing at us, and we thought they were making fun of us because we were a little gothed out that night. It turns out they were all huge fans of the show.

"We love your show!" they said. "Can we buy you dinner?"

"No, we're being fired," I told them. "Make these assholes pay for it!"

The last episode of *Oddities* aired on April 27, 2014. Then something odd happened. The show started airing on the streaming services and attracted a whole new crop of fans. Once it was on Netflix, a lot more people were able to see it. The irony is that *Oddities* became even more popular after it had been canceled.

That's when Regina was tuning in, and you know how that turned out.

Before *Oddities, Antiques Roadshow* was one of the first reality shows to feature rare and unusual antiques. It had a fairly conservative approach and a rigid format that put the focus squarely on the antiques that people brought in for evaluation. *Oddities* came along around the same time as *Pawn Stars* and *American Pickers*. What these shows had in common was that they put the focus on the people who were doing the buying and selling. *Oddities* stood out because even though the objects were unusual, the cast was entertaining, informative, and relatable.

Oddities showed the public a whole new way of collecting. People couldn't believe that the stuff being showcased on our show was actually worth money. The show generated a great deal of interest in the subculture of collecting oddities and inspired new collectors. There was a collecting scene before the show, but it was primarily underground. Because *Oddities* was on a major network, it brought this odd and unusual obsession into the mainstream. Suddenly you

MEMORABLE MOMENTS FROM ODDITIES

- *Going thrifting with model and embalmer Laura Flook*

- *Visiting Evan's Queen Anne Victorian home and getting to spend time with her beautifully curated collection*

- *Preparing a shrunken sloth head in my backyard in Brooklyn*

- *Traveling to LA and hanging out with Elvira*

Ryan with burlesque icon Dita Von Teese after filming an episode of *Oddities* at her home in Los Angeles

had stores like Obscura opening up around the country and all over the world. If you were a collector of oddities, you went from being part of a subculture to a member of a community.

It's fascinating to me that Instagram launched at virtually the same time as *Oddities*, making it easier than ever for amateur and professional collectors to share images of objects they wanted to showcase. Collectors could turn their Instagram page into their own cabinet of curiosities. Without physical limitations, the oddities collector community exploded. Suddenly, people were contacting me from all over the world.

Ryan with David Bowles, director of the TV show *Oddities*

"Hey, I saw you on the show. I've been looking for this particular item my whole life. Do you have one?"

"Actually, I have three."

It was all very good for business.

Oddities introduced this world to people who hadn't known it existed and created a community of people interested in exploring this passion. We made collecting oddities interesting and cool.

I think I stuck out because I was considerably younger than Mike and Evan. Evan had a pretty good home collection, meaning she had pieces that were part of her own private collection that she didn't intend to sell. Mike didn't have that. He was really good at finding stuff and selling it at the store. I had an excellent home collection, which *Oddities* helped showcase. And that helped inspire a new generation of collectors.

I know this because they tell me. To this day, young collectors come up to me and say they became interested in oddities because of the show and that I influenced their collections, which is still a very humbling thing to hear. I will forever be grateful to Mike and Evan for giving me that amazing opportunity and experience. They truly changed my life and even helped me refine my tastes. Together we helped make collecting oddities the phenomenon that it is today.

AFTER *ODDITIES*
Regina

My relationship with Ryan never would have worked out if *Oddities* hadn't been canceled.

Ryan's shooting schedule was six days a week, and he spent his one day off memorizing scripts. In addition, Discovery Channel was notorious for making the cast repeat, word for word, what they already said back to the camera during extensive interview sessions. The time commitment was demanding, and Ryan told me it was the one thing he hated about the show. With that kind of schedule, he wouldn't have had time for me, and that most likely would have been the end of us.

Without the show *Oddities*, our relationship evolved in a totally different way. For example, he never would have had the freedom to fly out to Paris with me if the show was still going. Not only was it the beginning of our obsession with traveling together, but those trips were crucial to our relationship and to Ryan's future.

In Paris, we had an epiphany.

While I was at work during the day, Ryan was free to wander around and imagine a new future for himself, and then at night we would meet up and explore Paris together. The museums we loved the most were small but lavish. They weren't the biggest museums, and they didn't have the most jaw-dropping collections, but they were meticulously curated and incredibly elaborate. Those museums really turned Ryan's whole aesthetic around.

"Let's make our house look like this," he'd say to me. "Let's turn the collection into *this*."

Up to that point, Ryan was collecting in a very masculine and, in my opinion, limited way. He had a highly developed aesthetic appreciation for a wide range of things, but after Paris his taste changed. He started to move away from these very structured and scientific presentations in favor of something more baroque. Ryan began to appreciate European antiques and artwork, things that were more layered and ornate.

I pointed out religious iconography to him and was surprised by how unfamiliar he was with it. I grew up in an intensely Catholic household, so I understood the layers of meaning. I don't think Ryan had ever set foot in a Gothic church before we went to Paris together. I desperately wanted to take him to Notre Dame, and he actually fought me on it.

"Nah, too touristy," he said.

"Are you kidding me?"

Finally, on one of the last trips we took to Paris while I was still working in the fashion industry, I dragged him down to Notre Dame. When I showed him the reliquaries, he got very excited. I couldn't wait to take him down to the chamber that showcased all the relics. I knew it was going to blow his freaking mind, and it did.

My situation was very different from Ryan's. I met him at the top of my career, and I was doing very well professionally as well as financially. Without *Oddities*, Ryan went back to buying and selling full time, and I often found myself envious of his lifestyle. He was constantly meeting with all these fascinating people in the collecting community. He'd have them over to the apartment, and they would stay up late into the night, sharing stories of their adventures. I, on the other hand, would have to go to bed so I could wake up early the next day for work.

I would ask myself, "Why am I working so hard for this company, making *them* all the money, when I could be working with Ryan?"

With his creativity and personality and my business background, I knew we would make a great team. It was just a matter of time before I figured out how to leave my six-figure job. From that point on, Ryan and I have been transforming our home into a place of wonder.

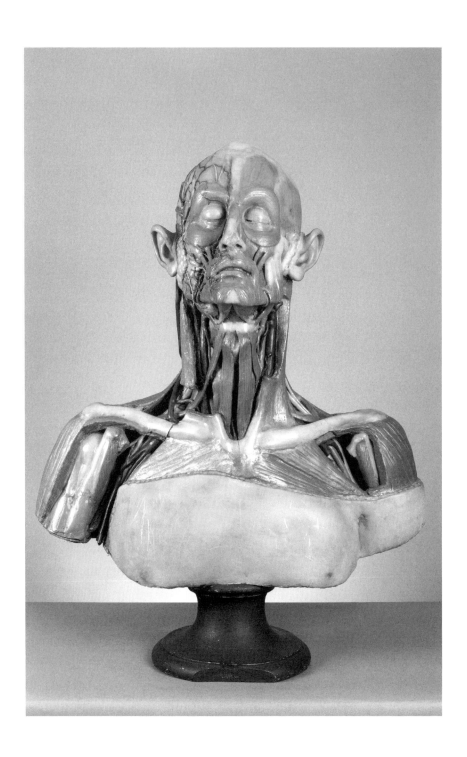

CHAPTER V

HOUSE *OF* *WAX*

CREEPY AND SOPHISTICATED

TROUBLE IN PARADISE

MAX WAX

HOUSE OF WAX

Regina's first communion in Cranston,
Rhode Island

CREEPY AND SOPHISTICATED
Regina

I never wanted a big, fancy wedding.

Contrary to what a lot of people think, I don't like being the center of attention. Because of the way I was raised, I have always felt much more comfortable behind the scenes. I grew up in a very strict, very Catholic household in Rhode Island. My parents had me later in life, and they were very old-fashioned. For example, on Good Friday my mom would make us shut off all the lights and didn't allow us to use any electricity. Good Friday was just one of the many religious days I dreaded throughout my childhood.

My interests were shaped by my older brother Matthew. I was always more interested in his toys, his friends, and especially his taste in music. My parents just didn't understand why I had to be so different from the sweet little girls in school. When my brother was out with his friends, I'd steal his CDs and rock out in my room. I got away with it for a while, but then one day my mom barged in and ripped all the hair metal posters off my wall and took away all the CDs. As if that weren't bad enough, she sent Matthew and me to church so the priests could tell us that what we were listening to was satanic. That's the kind of environment in which I was raised.

Naturally, I rebelled.

Looking back on my younger days, I realize I wasn't given a lot of tools for adulthood. Because my parents were so old-fashioned, they didn't sit me down and talk to me about going to college, having a career, or even dating. I was left to figure things out on my own.

Toward the end of high school, we moved to South Florida for my father's career. It was our third move since I'd started school, and I almost didn't graduate. Because my religion classes at Catholic school didn't transfer to public school, I had to make up the credits during the summer, and I didn't get to walk with my classmates during graduation.

Months later, the school mailed me my high school diploma. My grades weren't great, so I didn't bother applying for college. This wasn't something I discussed with my parents, who didn't offer much guidance one way or the other.

After modeling for a couple of years and hating it, I applied to become a flight attendant. I figured that if I was accepted, I'd have an instant career. I trained for six weeks in Moonship, Pennsylvania, and after I graduated from the training program, I was sent to Washington, DC, where I started a new life as a flight attendant. I worked for US Airways, and I flew for two years.

This is it, I thought. *This is my life.*

Then the unthinkable happened: 9/11.

Because I was young and didn't have much seniority, I was immediately furloughed until further notice. I had no choice but to pack my bags and head back to Florida. I figured I'd take a few months off and go back to work when the airline needed me. I had a great time—for a while. After a few months of goofing off, I realized the airline wasn't going to call me back. I had to find something else to do with my life.

I had become obsessed with a new upscale retail space called CityPlace in West Palm Beach that had all of these cool stores, including a brand-new Betsey Johnson boutique.

I thought Betsey Johnson was the coolest. She was a New York City fashion designer who had lived at the Chelsea Hotel, making clothes for Edie Sedgwick and hanging out with Andy Warhol. She was briefly married to John Cale of the Velvet Underground and was entrenched in the music scene. After she started her own line of clothing, she became famous for finishing her fashion shows with a crazy cartwheel and a split. She was a total icon who didn't take herself too seriously. I admired her.

Regina with her first mentor, Betsey Johnson, in West Palm Beach, Florida

I'd walk past the Betsey Johnson store and look at the cool girls standing outside the shop, smoking cigarettes in their amazing cupcake dresses. I felt like I had to work there. I was so bored waiting to go back to work as a flight attendant that one day I worked up the nerve to apply for a job.

"Hi! Are you hiring?"

The girl behind the counter said, "You can leave a résumé if you want," but her attitude read, "Please, you're never gonna get a job here."

I left my résumé, but no one called me. I waited and waited and then tried again a couple of months later. This time I talked to a much nicer girl. She took my résumé and said she'd give it to the manager. Luckily, I got a phone call to come in for an interview.

Although I had no experience in the fashion industry, my father worked in fashion all his life. Both he and my mother were very stylish and always wore beautiful clothes. I'd been to Fashion Week a few times, and I knew how to put myself together and carry myself. I stuck out in South Florida because I had a very different look than most girls my age. I much preferred wearing beautiful dresses and heels rather than cutoff jean shorts, tank tops, and sandals. I was offered a part-time job. It was the greatest thing that ever happened to me because within three months, I was managing the whole store.

I loved the brand. I loved the clothing. I found it easy to sell, especially when I wore the clothes and everybody wanted what I wore. Betsey was a dream boss. She was one of the first people to believe in me. She even helped me move to New York, where I would eventually flourish and have a long and successful career in the fashion industry. I owe her everything.

It was truly a happy accident. I went from working as a flight attendant to flying around the world in first class for my fashion career. Growing up, I was a misunderstood free spirit who flouted my parents' rules every chance I got, and here I was following in my father's footsteps in the fashion industry.

When Ryan and I got engaged, my parents were not doing well. My mother had been diagnosed with severe dementia, and my father was terminally ill. It was a very difficult time for my family.

After word of our engagement got out, a network reached out to us on social media to see if we'd be interested in being part of a new television show.

"Hey, guys, would you ever consider having your wedding on a TV show?"

We'd been looking for places in New York where we could hold the ceremony, and we weren't having much luck. My father was in a wheelchair, so the venue had to be accessible. I was saddened and surprised by how many places couldn't accommodate us. A lot of the venues that were wheelchair friendly were prohibitively expensive.

Ryan and I were paying for the ceremony ourselves and couldn't depend on my parents for financial assistance. In fact, I was taking care of most of their financial expenses. It was bad enough that my father wouldn't be able to walk me down the aisle and my mother wouldn't know what was going on, but then I started having nightmares about the wedding itself because I dreaded the thought of everyone looking at me.

When the network offered to plan the entire wedding and pick up the tab for most of the expenses, we didn't see how we could say no.

The show was called *Mikie Saves the Date*, and it was going to air on the FYI Channel. The premise of the show was that a famous wedding planner elevates ordinary weddings into big extravaganzas. I don't know how "ordinary" these weddings actually were, since many of the people involved were either rich or famous. We were neither. Our episode was going to be called "Creepy Sophistication." We were obviously going to be that season's weird wedding.

The producers scheduled our wedding for November, which was right around the corner. We wouldn't have picked a date that soon, but they wanted to shoot right away. We pushed for a Halloween wedding—what could be creepier and more sophisticated than that?—but they couldn't get the venue on that date.

As a result, we got married a lot faster than we'd originally planned, especially considering all the filming we had to do in advance of the show. When we sent out our wedding invitations, our friends and families thought we were crazy. They were happy that we had found each other, but I think they were a little taken aback by how fast everything was going.

"What the fuck, guys? Give it some time."

It was especially shocking to those closest to me. I had a wild past. I moved all over the place. My life was never stable. I had lots of boyfriends who were here today, gone tomorrow. A part of me thinks that my family was disappointed that I was finally settling down because my life was so entertaining to them. I was often the topic at family gatherings. Everyone wanted to know, "What's Regina up to now?"

What it was actually like filming a wedding for a reality TV show. Regina pulled out the big knife!

But not everyone was happy about our television wedding. I got an email from a family member who urged me to reconsider.

"You know, Regina, life is not a show."

I understood the concern, but I also felt as if I were racing against time so that my parents would be able to attend my wedding.

The ceremony was held on November 7, 2014, at the Foundry in Long Island City. It's literally an old iron foundry that looks like a Gothic dungeon, so it was perfect for us. The Foundry is a beautiful space but insanely expensive. We never would have been able to afford to get married there on our own.

Aesthetically, the wedding was stunning, but because we were filming a television show, we were separated for most of the day. Ryan was used to being on television, but it was a new experience for me. I was surrounded by total strangers, and I had microphones coming out of my corset and strapped to my thigh.

To be honest, I don't have a lot of happy memories from that day. Like most shoots, it was a long, uncomfortable day. I don't remember hanging out with Ryan at all. They kept us separate because they wanted footage from both the bride's and the groom's perspective, which was fine, but it came at the expense of us being able to enjoy our own wedding together. They didn't even think to put food aside for us. It's almost as if they forgot there was an actual couple getting married.

We invited all our friends and family to the wedding, including the coworker who had urged me to go on that first date with Ryan. We thought it would be funny to invite her to our wedding because if it weren't for her matchmaking instinct, we wouldn't have fallen in love. Ryan's old friend Mike Zohn, from Obscura, married us. Evan Michelson wasn't able to attend, but Andy Animal was there. He wanted to wear overalls with no shirt to the wedding. That would have been creepy but not sophisticated, and Ryan had to tell him to wear a suit. Andy complied but insisted on wearing motorcycle boots with it, which was fine by me.

Ultimately, the wedding wasn't what we thought it was going to be, but we didn't do it for us: We did it for my parents. If they had been healthy, it would have been a much simpler and more traditional affair. Even though my father didn't walk me down the aisle and couldn't stay for very long, he knew that I was going to be okay. That was important to me, but also heartbreaking. Our wedding was the last trip he would ever take, and he passed away a short while afterward.

In retrospect, if I had to do it all over again, I'd do it all differently. I can say the same thing for our honeymoon.

TROUBLE IN PARADISE
Ryan

W e didn't go on our honeymoon immediately after our wedding. We were insanely busy, and because so much of the
wedding was out of our control, we decided to postpone our honeymoon until the spring, when we'd have time to really enjoy it. At least,
that was the plan.

We hired a travel agency to plan our trip to Hawai'i down to the
last detail so that everything would be perfect. The past year had been
a whirlwind, and we needed to get away from it all for a while. No
TV producers, no collectors, no clients. Just the two of us.

Then I received a phone call from out of the blue that had the
potential to change our lives. A representative of a private collector
in Europe informed me that a collection of wax figures was going up
for sale. Was I interested?

The term *wax figures* conjures up images of cheap renditions
of Hollywood celebrities in wax museums that are little more than
tourist traps. But it wasn't always this way. Before the advent of film,
television, and digital technology, the best method for creating a
lifelike representation of a human form was with wax. Wax was one
of the few materials that had the potential to capture the beauty of
the human figure *and* stand the test of time—if it was handled safely.
To the untrained eye, wax models were macabre, but I found them
incredibly beautiful.

So, yes, I was very interested.

The middleman told me he would send over photographs of the
collection, and we set up a meeting for later in the week. The images
arrived the next morning. When I started going through the photos,
I nearly fell out of my chair. The word *collection* didn't do justice to

this lot. There were enough figures to fill an entire museum. There seemed to be no end to the images.

Two things were clear: This was going to cost a lot of money, and it was going to take some time to pull together the financing. Time was exactly what I didn't have on my side because I was scheduled to leave for Hawai'i in a few days. I went into the meeting with the middleman hoping I could buy some time, but he had other ideas.

"You have forty-eight hours to tell me if you want this collection," he said. "I've got another client who is showing a great deal of interest. So you have two days to make an offer."

This was on a Friday, and we were supposed to leave on our honeymoon on Sunday. Rescheduling our trip to Hawai'i was unthinkable. I had to make a spur-of-the-moment decision, except this wasn't a $10,000 deal. This collection was easily worth half a million dollars. It was also located in Munich, Germany, which added to the complexity. Nothing about this deal would be easy.

"I'll see what I can do," I said.

I now had a few days to figure out how the hell to make this work. First, I needed to find a buyer to partner with. I wanted to buy the entire collection myself and then figure out what to do with it later, but it was much too expensive for that. So I had to come up with a buyer. I had a little bit of an inkling of what I was going to do and how I was going to do it, but it involved constant communication with a handful of people, and I only had a few hours to work the phones before the banks closed and people got started with their weekends.

I typically never use investors. I always try to do things within my budget. I learned pretty early in my career that it's better when you don't have to rely on others. If a collection costs more than I can handle on my own, I usually scrap the deal.

But in this business, you have to be flexible. When someone comes along with a once-in-a-lifetime opportunity, you have to find a way to make it work. In this case, I needed an investor, even if it meant losing a lot of the profits or owing people money. Over the years, I've bought most of the collections that have been offered to me, even when I was close to broke. Ironically, the few that I turned down were wax collections from Europe. The price was too steep or the cost of shipping the collection overseas made it prohibitive. I was determined not to let this one slip away.

Initially, we approached some high-end collectors who are major players in the world of horror, including Guillermo del Toro, Eli Roth, and Rob Zombie, some of whom we'd worked with before. They were all intrigued, and they each identified favorite pieces from the collection, but in the end it came down to the same thing every time: They had no clue what they'd do with a collection of that size.

"What the hell am I going to do with two hundred wax statues?" Guillermo said to me over the phone.

No one disputed that it was a great collection, but no one had the space for it. The thing that made the collection special also made it challenging to sell. Each person that we showed it to passed. Meanwhile, we were getting down to the wire because our forty-eight-hour deadline was approaching.

Finally, we had a lead. A friend who was an executive in the music industry and who knew lots of collectors and high rollers reached out and said she wanted to introduce someone to us. His name was Tim League, the founder of the Alamo Drafthouse Cinema, a theater chain that originated in Texas and served food and drinks during screenings. League was the visionary behind a lot of the interesting things that Alamo Drafthouse Cinema has to offer, like screening films at the locations where they were shot and designing beautifully curated bars inside the movie theater lobbies.

I thought it was ironic that League was interested in the collection since wax museums were precursors to the moving image. It was the rising popularity of cinema that turned wax museums into relics of the past. People wanted to go to the movies, not a dusty old museum.

I showed him photos of the collection, and he was intrigued. We negotiated a little bit and agreed on a ballpark figure, but he needed more time to think about it, which probably meant he wanted to run the numbers.

I called the middleman and told him that we had a potential buyer but that I was getting on an airplane to go on my honeymoon. He told us he'd let the collector know, but if another offer came along, they'd have to sell it. I couldn't let that happen. I'd never seen anything as extensive and beautiful as this collection.

One of the only moments of relaxation in between negotiations during the honeymoon in Kaua'i, Hawai'i

Perhaps most importantly, a collection of this size was incredibly rare because so many European wax figures from this period were destroyed during the two world wars with Germany.

The flight to Hawai'i was extremely long, and I used the time to do as much research as I could.

Most of the wax figures in the collection had been part of a popular German museum called Castan's Panopticum that operated between 1869 and 1922, making some of the structures over 150 years old. Castan's was a predecessor of, and then a rival to, Madame Tussaud's Wax Museum in London and was known throughout Europe.

The wax sculptures depicted everything from anatomical figures to medical abnormalities, serial killers to famous people of the time. There were also a large number of death masks and moulages in the collection, including casts from ethnographic studies. Most of these pieces were created before the rise of photography and the subsequent explosion of moving images. For many audiences, Castan's Panopticum was their first opportunity to see representations of people from different cultures and other historical eras in three dimensions.

The Panopticum was designed to appeal to a broad audience—at its peak the exhibit would bring in five thousand people a day—but the curators always showcased its educational benefits. Although Castan's employed the most skilled modelers, many of whom were trained anatomists whose work was used to instruct medical students, the atmosphere at Castan's Panopticum could be as salacious as a carnival sideshow.

The more I learned about the history of the wax figures, many of which were life-size, the more I wanted to get my hands on them.

As soon as we landed in Kaua'i, we received good news: League had accepted my proposal.

"Go ahead and do it!" he said.

I took a deep breath and called the middleman, hoping the collection hadn't been sold out from underneath us.

"The collection is yours," he said.

It would have been nice if that was that, but deals of this size involve near-constant communication between all parties. A million questions come up that have to be answered right away, or the deal can fall apart. The seller needs assurances about the financing, the investors need assurances about the collection, and the banks need assurances about everything. The fact that I was in Hawai'i, my partners were in New York, and the client was in Germany made

everything that much more challenging. I was afraid that the second
I stopped paying attention, some private collector with deep pockets
was going to swoop in and snatch it away from us.

The problem was that I was supposed to be relaxing and enjoying
my honeymoon, not stressing out over a $500,000 deal. It wasn't a
good situation, and Regina wasn't happy about it.

In fact, she was pissed.

———◆◆◆———

MAX WAX
Regina

"What the fuck have I done with my life?"

I was lying on the beach, cursing up a storm.

We'd specifically booked a trip to Kaua'i so we'd be as far away
from our regular lives as possible, and here I was all alone on my
honeymoon. Cell service was so bad on the island that the only place
we could make or take calls was in our hotel room. Ryan was insanely
distracted and spent the first few days pacing our room. Every time I
encouraged him to get out and do something for a few minutes, he'd
say, "I'm waiting on a call" or "I need to take this call."

For days it felt like we were living in limbo, one missed call away
from the deal falling through.

That wasn't how I imagined spending my honeymoon, and I'd
had enough.

So I went to the beach—by myself.

After a few hours alone, Ryan finally got the message that I was
here to have fun—with or without him—and I was able to coax him
out of the hotel so we could explore Kaua'i. I wanted to rent a car
and go for a drive around the island, but there weren't many rental

cars available on such short notice. The only vehicle available was a Toyota Corolla. We took it and set out on an adventure.

We quickly found out why it was the last car on the lot: It wasn't equipped for the dirt roads of the island's interior. Somehow we ended up getting the Corolla stuck in a pond in the middle of the jungle.

Of course, that's when the call we'd been waiting for came through.

"Hello?" Ryan said.

A garbled voice came over the line. The connection was patchy, and Ryan couldn't make out what the person on the other end was saying.

"I'll call you back!" Ryan said and hung up the phone.

We got out of the car, which was now covered in both frogs and slime. We trekked down to the beach, where we had one bar of service. Instead of calling for help, Ryan called New York to talk to League.

The last piece of the financing had gone through. We were finally able to enjoy our honeymoon—what was left of it, anyway—but little did I know that our adventure was just getting started.

Back in New York, we had just enough time to shake the sand out of our suitcases and sleep for a few hours before we had to pack our bags again. This time we were headed in the other direction, across the Atlantic Ocean to Munich, Germany.

Our offer had been accepted and a deal was in place, but we still hadn't seen the collection in person. So far, all we'd seen were images. The pieces had been expertly photographed, which was very helpful when Ryan was doing his research, but you can't make a $500,000 investment based on a few photos.

It takes a sophisticated eye to be able to assess the value of a collection from photographs, but obviously a picture can't tell the whole story. We needed to see each model from every angle—especially since we were dealing with wax. Normally, we would check out the collection first and figure out what to do from there. This was a unique situation where we'd made an offer without actually seeing the items. We needed to go to Germany and inspect the collection and make sure it was everything the middleman said it was.

We arrived in Munich jet-lagged and exhausted. We'd taken an overnight flight, and I had a few glasses of wine on the plane, which knocked me out. I woke up groggy and disoriented, badly in need of coffee. I don't think I've even been that tired. I was basically sleep-walking.

We cleared customs and made our way outside the terminal to meet our ride. Because the collector spoke in broken English, Ryan had mostly dealt with the middleman, so it was somewhat surprising to learn that the collector himself would be picking us up at the airport. We offered to take a taxi to his estate, but the collector, whom we'll call Max Wax, insisted on meeting us in person.

Even though we'd never met him before, we had no trouble spotting him in the airport parking lot. He was the one standing next to a tiny car and waving a wax arm.

I thought I was hallucinating.

Max Wax was a large, hulking man who was a big player in Europe's antiquarian community. He also valued his privacy, so there wasn't a whole lot about him on the internet. He was a complete mystery to us, which was odd considering we were going to do a huge deal with him.

We introduced ourselves to Max, who seemed very nice. Despite his bulk, he had an aristocratic bearing. He also had the smallest car

I've ever seen. I think it was a Fiat. We crammed our luggage into the trunk and piled into the car with Ryan sitting in the front next to Max and me wedged into the back.

Max's estate was about an hour and a half outside of Munich, but we didn't know that at the time. Max was a crazy driver who got that Fiat up to 100 miles per hour on multiple occasions. I basically accepted the fact that we were going to die, but I was so tired I didn't really care. I thought I must be exaggerating the situation, but when Ryan reached back from the front seat to squeeze my hand, I realized he was just as scared as I was.

All right, I thought, *we've finally done ourselves in here. This is how we're going to die.*

I was drifting in and out of consciousness and having really weird dreams. Every time I woke up, we were racing deeper into the Black Forest. I could hear Ryan talking to Max in the front seat, but I had no idea what they were saying or where we were going. The trip seemed to take forever, but I didn't know if Max lived a few minutes or several hours away. We raced through small, ancient villages that felt like something out of a fairy tale. I was never really sure if I was dreaming or not.

We finally pulled over in a tiny town with cobblestone streets, and Max took us to lunch. Everyone in the village knew him, and the food at the restaurant was delicious. Throughout the meal, people kept coming up to our table and shaking Max's hand. I started to feel a little bit better about the situation.

After lunch, which included some wine, we climbed into the car, and I immediately fell asleep. Before too long we rolled up to a gigantic Bavarian estate that looked like it was under construction.

"Okay, let's go look at the collection," Max said as soon as we walked in the front door. "It's down in the basement!"

Of course it was in a basement. We'd traveled all the way to Germany to go poke around in another musty basement.

Max opened the door, and we descended into a giant, cavern-like room. There were crates everywhere, about two hundred in all. Each crate had been custom-built for the wax figure it held. There was a separate room, off to the side, where some of the larger pieces were stored. It didn't feel like a storage room, though, because Max had fabulous antiques scattered around the room. I felt as if I were on a movie set.

We were dumbfounded by the vastness of the collection. Ryan said he'd never seen so many anatomical wax antiques in one place before. He'd purchased one or two pieces over the years, but they tend to be really expensive because of how rare they are. The truly valuable moulages just don't come up for sale very often.

Items from Max Wax's collection in a murky basement outside of Munich, Germany. These moulages would later end up in the House of Wax collection.

Few private collections include wax figures because of the challenge of maintaining them. You can't put them on a shelf and forget about them. They can't be too hot, or they'll melt, obviously, but the real threat is the cold. If a wax figure gets too cool, it will become brittle and break. It's much more common for wax figures to be damaged from the cold than from the heat. You have to care for them almost as if they were people, and most collectors—at least the ones we know—prefer dead things to the living. In this case, the wax figures were meant to simulate life and had received the utmost attention and care.

We went through the collection, and I could tell the pieces were good because Ryan was super excited. In fact, the collection was even larger than we had thought because some of the figures hadn't been included in the photo gallery. A good chunk of the negotiations were dedicated to the cost of the shipping, which was easily a quarter of the total amount. Each item was packed in its own crate, and some of them were life-size models. Plus, the collection had to be shipped on a vessel that was temperature-controlled.

After some back-and-forth, we struck a deal.

As we were wrapping things up, Max asked me in his unusual accent, "Would you like a preserved penis?"

"Um, sure?" I said, unsure of the etiquette in this situation.

Max handed me a jar. Inside was a perfectly preserved wax model of a penis. That was our wedding gift from Max Wax.

We went out to dinner with Max and his lovely wife, and then they dropped us off at our hotel. We slept until late in the afternoon the following day. We woke up, ate sausages, drank some beer—as one does in Munich—and then flew back to New York. It was the craziest seventy-two hours of my entire life.

Somehow everything worked out, but as far as I'm concerned, Ryan still owes me a trip to Hawai'i.

HOUSE OF WAX
Ryan & Regina

The collection we bought from Max Wax arrived at the port a few months later. We had the items shipped to a storage facility in Brooklyn where we had a pair of large storage units. These were just two of five units we used to store everything that wouldn't fit into our Greenpoint apartment. We had a total of four units in Brooklyn and another one in New Jersey.

They weren't all full, but we've learned from experience to try and keep pieces together—especially if they're from the same collection. For instance, we bought a nineteenth-century apothecary from a drugstore that went out of business. We put all that stuff in one storage unit. That was the best way for us to keep track of the various items in that collection. Sometimes we have periods where we're not buying anything and have time to organize things. Sometimes we're buying all the time and don't want to get the pieces mixed up in different collections. If you're not organized, things can get lost, and it just makes life difficult.

The crates showed up in massive trucks. From the look of things, we were going to need a bigger storage unit. Luckily, the storage facility had a forklift and, with the help of some assistants, we unloaded all of the crates from the trucks and moved them into the storage units. It took all day because we had to offload each crate and inspect the piece before letting the shipping company driver leave. Incredibly, not a single piece was damaged in transit, which was truly a miracle.

We informed League that his wax models had arrived safe and sound, and he shared his plans for the collection. He wanted to showcase the figures in a museum inside Alamo Drafthouse's brand-new downtown Brooklyn location.

"It will be a museum inside of a bar where we can throw events, have parties, and guests can check out the wax sculptures. Would you two be interested in curating the exhibition?"

We didn't even have to think about it.

Of course we were interested.

Most Alamo Drafthouse locations have a bar in or adjacent to the lobby, and each bar has its own theme. For instance, there's one in Staten Island called the Flying Guillotine, a kung fu–themed bar designed in part by RZA of the Wu-Tang Clan.

The downtown Brooklyn location was a bit different because it was in a building that shared space with companies like Century 21, Trader Joe's, and Target, so it had a very corporate vibe.

We wanted to replicate what we thought Castan's Panopticum would have looked like, which meant taking guests back into the nineteenth century. We gave it a Victorian feel with red velvet curtains, faux-gas chandeliers, and elaborate wallpaper. All of the wax anatomical structures were safely ensconced in glass cabinets that we designed. We wanted it to feel like you're in a museum, except you could have an alcoholic beverage. We put a great deal of thought into everything—even the labels that accompanied each of the waxworks. We wanted each sculpture to tell a story and give its history.

The centerpiece of the collection is a pair of wax models depicting different ways in which a woman gives birth. These were made by the famous wax maker E. E. Hammer. Among wax collectors, Hammer's moulages are probably the most sought-after. They are striking pieces. We can't think of another space where you can have a drink and look at not one, but two anatomical models of women giving birth.

League gave us carte blanche to do what we wanted, and we didn't spare any expense. On the stage, we arranged a large display of genitalia ravaged by syphilis that could be concealed by a curtain if needed and a somewhat controversial wall of fetal abnormalities. We

called the museum House of Wax as an homage to the classic horror
film starring Vincent Price as a wax sculptor with a terrifying secret.

It took a long time to get the space together because it was such
a monstrosity and we ran into
many delays. It truly was a labor
of love. We cocurated the space
and had an assistant execute the
signage and labeling. It was supposed to be done in four months,
but it took over a year.

When House of Wax opened,
we did a lot of press junkets and
gave tours. We'd explain the history of the museum and of the
individual pieces. Before long,
medical schools started to visit,
which was fascinating because
that's why these types of preparations were made in the first
place. Although the models were
made for the medical community,

Opening night of House of Wax.
Brooklyn, NYC.

Castan's was a place of entertainment—because who doesn't want to
look at a wax figure with two penises?

To help spread the word about House of Wax and to make sure
the right people found out about it, we threw some of the coolest
parties on the planet. We did an absinthe night that got pretty wild
with our friends from the Green Fairy and the No Ring Circus. We
curated a fashion show at the museum for Ashley Rose Couture. We
hosted an art show with our friends Mothmeister from Belgium,
a lecture about magick by Damien Echols of the West Memphis
Three, and a book launch for porn star Stoya. We wanted to bring in

people who were cultural icons outside the margins of mainstream entertainment.

Not everyone was a fan of the museum.

Some people were offended by some of the ethnographic sculptures, complaining that they reflected cultural stereotypes. One person was horrified by the fetal abnormalities on display and wrote a scathing review. It's a corporate space, so we made sure to post a disclaimer about the museum's contents to everyone who came inside.

For the most part, people loved what we'd created because it was different. We frequently witnessed couples on their first date at House of Wax. They would use the museum as a litmus test. If you were willing to go on a second date after spending time with graphic anatomical models, then you were cool!

We believe in doing things the right away. We know people who will spend all kinds of energy looking for loopholes and trying to beat the system.

That's not us. We're too busy for that.

In our experience, taking shortcuts usually ends up costing you in the long run. But you have to be careful. There have been times when our failure to read a contract carefully bit us in the ass. We've learned that it's always easier to ask for changes before you sign the contract than afterward. So now we have lawyers and legal experts pore over all of our contracts. Sometimes, no matter how careful you are, you still gotta pay the man.

For example, about six months after we bought the collection from Max Wax, we got a bill in the mail for $60,000. We immediately started freaking out. We called our lawyer and asked him to figure out what was going on.

"What the hell is this? Didn't we already pay taxes on this?"

"Let me talk to the broker," he said.

HIGHLIGHTS OF HOUSE OF WAX

- *Waxwork sculptures of women giving birth*
- *Death mask of Kaiser Wilhelm I*
- *Display of genital deformities*
- *Wax heads of historical figures from around the world*
- *Life-size model of the digestive tract*
- *A fellow from Deutschland with a pair of penises*

Anatomical preparations from House of Wax, above, showing the effects of corsetry on the internal organs of a woman (the one on the right by the famed anatomist and wax maker E. E. Hammer), and left, showcasing different parts of the body affected by leprosy

When you're shipping overseas, you have to use a shipping broker to navigate all of the international rules and regulations that govern where you're shipping from and where you're shipping to. There are duties and fees and taxes and tariffs to pay, and there's no way you can do it yourself without getting bogged down and making a mistake. You have to go through proper legal channels in those situations, and there are a lot of them.

Because the wax figures were over 150 years old, there was an additional level of red tape to sort through. Our lawyer checked all the paperwork and assured us there wouldn't be any holdups at the port. And there weren't any. The shipment went through without issues, quickly and efficiently.

The bill came from the port of New York. They basically said, "Fuck you. We're taking a cut." There was nothing we could do about it. We had an entire legal team review the paperwork, but they couldn't find a thing.

"Sorry, we're gonna have to pay this."

"We" meaning "us."

We've scuttled deals for less. When you purchase a collection, you weigh the price of each piece and what it's going to cost to ship it and store it, and then you try to determine if you'll be able to turn a profit. Tacking on an extra $60,000 charge on top blows those calculations out of the water.

Recently, we were considering purchasing the contents of a museum in Majorca, Spain. One of the reasons why we didn't go through with it is because if the collection got stuck at customs, it could jack up the price beyond our ability to pay for it. Even if we filed the proper paperwork, if a customs agent says, "I think these items have mites" or "This specimen is marked incorrectly," then the entire shipment is denied entry. When your shipment is held up at customs, they charge you rent for every day that it's stuck there. How long that takes is not up to you. You're completely at the mercy of the customs agents. They determine how long it will have to sit there, and the situation usually doesn't get resolved until money changes hands.

I have friends who bought taxidermy collections from foreign countries that got held up at customs because they needed additional paperwork. Those collections sat and sat, and there was nothing they could do about it. In one instance, a friend ended up paying an additional $150,000. It's a huge risk that you have to take into consideration when buying from collectors overseas.

Knowing what we know now, would we do the Max Wax deal again?

Absolutely.

We put House of Wax on the map with that collection. All the hustle, all the work, and all the fees paid off, and people still talk about how cool it is. It's like a strange slice of the Old Country in downtown Brooklyn. In exchange for cocurating the museum, we took equity in the Alamo Drafthouse Cinema. We have a piece of House of Wax, and best of all, we got to play with all the toys in Castan's Panopticum.

CHAPTER VI

THE
HELPING HAND

THE HAUNTED MUSEUM
WELCOME TO THE DOLLHOUSE
THE EYE
THE CREEPY COFFINS

A gang of Charlie McCarthy dolls purchased several years ago. All were sold except for two.

THE HAUNTED MUSEUM
Ryan & Regina

"Is any of this stuff haunted?"

That's usually the first question that people ask when they come to our house and take a look at our collection. Collectors rarely ask this question. It's usually a layperson or a reporter who's looking for an angle for a story. But we get this question all the time from our friends and acquaintances too.

It's not an easy question to answer.

"Sure," we say.

Then we go from room to room and point out all the pieces that are purported to be haunted. It's a fairly lengthy list. We have plenty of objects associated with the paranormal—from books to relics to weapons—but there's a difference between a piece that's been documented as haunted and one that has actually exhibited uncanny behavior.

We feel you have to believe that something is haunted for a ghost or spirit to present itself. In other words, you have to be open to the possibility of the supernatural. It's rare that we have experienced those types of phenomena.

That said, a few items from our collection do have an unusual energy about them. For instance, we recently sold a straitjacket from the '40s or '50s that was used at Bellevue Hospital, from which more than a few horror stories have emerged over the years. The piece is unusually heavy considering it's made of fabric. Thankfully, we won't be tempted to try that item on for size anytime soon.

Sterling silver vanity mirror that the previous owner alleged to be haunted

We also have a mirror that used to hang in another New York City mental hospital that is supposedly haunted—or so we've been told. It's certainly creepy looking. The reflective material on the back of antique mirrors was typically made with mercury. If you scratch it off, you can see through the clear glass of the mirror. When this substance begins to deteriorate and darken, sometimes you'll see a blackened patina in places where the mirror no longer reflects your image. This particular mirror has strange patterns and is fabulously macabre, though we're not exactly sure of its provenance.

We own another mirror that is supposedly haunted. This one's a Victorian hand mirror. It's made of sterling silver and would originally have been part of a vanity set. The mercury-based glass mirror is very deteriorated. On the silver casing is an embossed vampire bat with lots of intricate filigree. The seller told me after we purchased it that it was haunted, and we're starting to believe her. It certainly looks spooky and possesses a strange sort of energy when we peer into the mirror.

Also in our possession is a dagger constructed for the purpose of extracting the soul from a witch. We found it in a large collection we purchased; the previous owner had passed away, so we couldn't ask questions about it, but what little paperwork we were able to find indicates that it is a handwrought iron dagger from the seventeenth century. It's not terribly sharp, and there are no real markings on it, so there's no way to tell if it was ever used (i.e., if it's a murder weapon).

We're intrigued by the story, which is what makes this item unique, but does the dagger really steal the souls of witches? Probably not—unless you believe it does. That's the power of a good story.

We also have an extensive collection of rare, antique books, many of which deal with the occult. They are predominantly from the fourteenth to nineteenth centuries, and their subject matter ranges from anatomy to natural history, mathematics to witchcraft, which has been our main focus in recent years.

Last year we picked up a very old book called *The Magus* by Francis Barrett. A magus, or mage, was a male sorcerer or magician who was adept in the art of celestial intelligence. This volume was produced in 1801 and is one of the more comprehensive books on

A very unassuming seventeenth-century dagger said to be used to extract the soul from a witch

witchcraft from that era. It was read by all sorts of people who were interested in the science of natural magic and is highly sought-after today.

We managed to find one of the original copies with a gilded dragon on the spine and a marbled cover. It's quite beautiful, but what makes this particular edition remarkable are the thirteen hand-painted watercolor plates. The illustrations themselves are quite grotesque and feature images of demons known as the Vessels of Wrath. Most copies available today don't have the plates. Collectors removed the illustrations and sold them separately because they are so valuable. Of course, we've never tried to summon any of the demons described in the book, but anything is possible.

There's no question about it: We've got plenty of objects that check all the boxes in the haunted category. We have bought things at flea markets and antique shows that the dealers said were haunted, but we haven't experienced any unusual phenomena with them ourselves. Sellers often make such claims to drive the price up or to make a piece more attractive to a certain type of buyer.

The simple fact of the matter is that people are drawn to things that have a story attached to them. An unusual occurrence. A historical footnote. A whiff of celebrity. For example, if we're selling something that came from Billy Jamieson's collection, we always mention it because he was one of the best collectors that ever lived. Jamieson is so well known in collecting circles that it would be bad business to not mention him. It gives the piece a bit more legitimacy knowing that it passed through the hands of someone who is thought of as an expert.

We don't know if people think of us in the same way, but we know for a fact that people want to own things that were once part of our collection. They say that if we owned it, there must be something to it, a reason that it attracted our attention and compelled us to buy it.

Putting too much faith in a story is a good way to get bamboozled. It can lead you to be attracted to something you might not otherwise be interested in. For example, let's say you have an item like an old Victorian cape that's worth $1,000. If that item was previously owned by Edgar Allan Poe, you could easily get much more for it. Attaching his name to the item makes it more interesting and more valuable.

Poe, however, died a long time ago. There are a finite number of objects in the world that he owned. He's not buying any more capes, and if a seller claims to have one that Poe owned, chances are it's a fake. Unless you're an expert in Victorian-era capes favored by eccentric nineteenth-century writers, you're going to regret the purchase. If you are an expert in textiles from that era, then you'll enjoy owning the cape regardless of its provenance.

Authenticating the supernatural is impossible, but a lot of people make the assumption that because they had an experience with an object or a place, others will too. We don't necessarily agree with that theory. We think if you believe in something strongly enough, you can manifest it in the right circumstances. People do that with religion all the time. "God saved me!" Well, maybe, but what if it was a coincidence?

Maybe you did something subconsciously to help yourself out of a difficult situation. Maybe others helped you out without your knowledge. Whatever the case may be, we don't believe in divine intervention. More often than not, what some people view as "magical" or "spiritual" is just a narrative they've created around coincidence. The most logical explanation is most likely to be true.

That's how we tend to think about life. We don't know if that's right or wrong, but it's the way we feel. We're certainly open to seeing evidence of paranormal activities. Having not experienced anything terribly specific at this point in our lives and having dealt in this kind of material for so long, we're losing our ability to believe. We've been in abandoned mental institutions, old prisons, places where grotesque and heinous acts of violence have happened, places where hundreds—if not thousands—of unthinkable crimes have been committed, places you'd definitely think would be haunted, but we haven't experienced a thing.

So we're a little skeptical.

Do you believe in ghosts?

Great! Tell us your stories, especially if they pertain to haunted objects. Like most people, we love hearing those stories. It just so happens that we've never had an undeniable encounter with the supernatural. You would think that, considering the types of objects that we deal with, *something* would have happened to us by now, but it hasn't.

However, we've had a couple of encounters we're unsure about, where things occurred that we can't quite explain: experiences that blur the line between a rational explanation and the uncanny. Let us tell you about a few of them.

— ❖ —

WELCOME TO THE DOLLHOUSE
Ryan

Let's make one thing perfectly clear: I *want* to be haunted. I'm not a nonbeliever, nor do I have any issues with people who believe in the paranormal.

It would probably help my career, actually. When we go to a TV pitch meeting, the producers almost always ask us the same question: "Would you guys do a paranormal show?"

The answer, of course, is no because we would be lying if we said, "Yes, all this stuff is haunted."

We could open up our house as a haunted museum and get filthy rich. I get it. It's like having a mummy in a museum. It sells tickets. But it wouldn't be true, and the next thing you know these producers would have us tracking down spirits in supposedly haunted houses, and all of our credibility as antiquarians would go out the window. There are already at least a dozen of those shows on television. Every network has one, sometimes more than one. It's absolutely absurd.

That's not who we are or what we're about. Ultimately, "going paranormal" would damage our reputations.

Ryan in the room dedicated to the dolls in the collection

Nevertheless, I love getting my hands on something with a creepy story attached to it. I'm not talking about murder memorabilia. We steer clear of those types of items. We find them to be in poor taste and disrespectful to the victims' families. We're interested in objects where you can tell just by looking at them that there's a story to be told. Sometimes all it takes is one look and I *have* to know everything about it. Even then, I treat it like any other object. Whether it's ghosts or religion, show me the facts.

There is, however, an object in my collection—two objects really— that I've had unusual experiences with that I'm not quite able to explain. I'm not even sure how to talk about it, to be perfectly honest.

It involves dolls.

I've been fascinated with dolls all my life. When I was a kid, G.I. Joe figures were really popular. I loved playing with them, and I had several different types. They came in different skin tones and hair colors and Army outfits, but they were all the same: 4-inch dolls made of molded plastic with jointed limbs held together by a single screw and elastic bands.

I was always interested in the insides of things, so it was only a matter of time before I started fiddling with the screw and realizing I could take G.I. Joe's body apart and put him back together in different ways. I'd take one doll's head and put it on a different body with different arms and legs. Then I'd bring my mutant G.I. Joes to school, and everyone thought it was the coolest thing ever.

Naturally, I started creating these specialized little G.I. Joe dolls that no one else had. If one of my friends wanted a customized doll, I'd sell it to them or trade for normal G.I. Joes that I could use to make more custom dolls. I was like a mad scientist disassembling different dolls and putting them back together in my own way.

I think my parents thought I might be gay because one year I asked for a Barbie doll for my birthday. I wanted the one that came with a horse. She was a very pretty and feminine Barbie, but I had other intentions. Instead of creating a serene stable where Barbie would ride her cute little horse off into the sunset, I was going to take the dolls apart and draw on them and turn Barbie and her horse into a cyborg death machine. Strange, maybe, but not queer.

Anyway, if you were to do an inventory of my collection today, you'd find that a large percentage of my most treasured pieces are, technically, dolls. For instance, I'm obsessed with cage dolls. A cage doll is a figure whose upper portion resembles the head and torso of a human. The rest of the structure is a pedestal that looks like a cage. This lower portion was typically covered by a gown or religious garment and wasn't meant to be seen. When you remove the clothes, these dolls are quite peculiar looking. They date back to the sixteenth

RYAN'S FAVORITE "DOLLS"

- *Eighteenth-century santos cage doll from Spain*

- *Seventeenth-century polychrome reliquary bust*

- *Statue of a naked demon with a pitchfork picking its nose*

- *Numerous vintage artist mannequins in a variety of sizes*

- *Two restless and possibly haunted Charlie McCarthy ventriloquist dummies*

century and were used in smaller churches or chapels or on home altars to depict a saint or holy figure.

I was always interested in cage dolls, but I didn't own one until about ten years ago. That purchase led me down the path to learning everything I could about them: when they were used, who originally made them, and when antiquarians started collecting them.

It's one thing to see a piece in a collection or even a museum, but actually having one in your possession and being able to spend more time with it is what takes collecting to another level. It allows you to become intimate with a piece in a way that isn't possible when you're looking at it from a distance. That, more than anything, is what sparks my curiosity and cultivates a sense of wonder.

I've come to accept my obsession with dolls, but instead of Barbies and G.I. Joe figures, now I collect high-end dolls. This brings us to a pair of very unusual dolls in my collection, and they both happen to be Charlie McCarthy ventriloquist dummies.

It took over forty years, but thanks to these two early Charlie McCarthy dolls the collection has finally become haunted. Note the open mouth on the doll on the left. It kept falling out continuously during the photo shoot. This was the first time this happened since they were purchased several years ago.

The story goes that over a hundred years ago a ventriloquist named Edgar Bergen took a sketch of an Irish newspaper boy to a woodcarver and asked him to make a dummy for his act. Bergen named the dummy Charlie McCarthy, and together they had a long career spanning five decades. The act was so popular that it spawned a line of ventriloquist dummies that were all identical copies of Charlie McCarthy.

When you hear the term *ventriloquist dummy*, the image of Charlie McCarthy probably springs into your head. With a white face, rosy cheeks, and bright red lips, the dolls are often decked out in a suit with a top hat and a monocle. Vintage Charlie McCarthy dolls are very rare—especially when they're in good condition.

Ventriloquist dummies have been fodder for horror movies for decades. Every year there's a new movie or sequel about a doll with supernatural powers. There's even an apocryphal story about a ventriloquist who used a dead child in place of a dummy for his act.

This story has been repeated so many times that it's practically an urban legend. There's something about these talking dolls whose masters bring them to life that has infiltrated the darkest corners of our imaginations.

A few years ago, we purchased a collection of twelve Charlie McCarthy dolls from an antiques dealer in Connecticut with whom I've become friends. Although oddities aren't his forte, he will give us a call when he has something he thinks we might like. He told us the dolls were sold to him by the original collector.

He said the collector told him: "These little people need to go to a home where they can thrive and have the space they need to live."

I didn't think much of that statement at the time, but I've thought about his words quite a bit since then.

I sold most of the collection but kept what I considered to be the best two. I displayed them in my library, where they sat on a leather chair like a pair of perfectly behaved gentleman, waiting for a ventriloquist to come along and bring them back to life.

Well, apparently these little dummies weren't happy with this arrangement because they had a strange habit of moving around.

The first time it happened, I was annoyed. I always left the dolls in the same place and the same position, so it was a bit of a shock to find one of them seated on a different chair.

"Did you move my ventriloquist dolls?" I asked Regina.

"No, Ryan," she said, "I don't play with your dolls."

We have housekeepers who help with the cleaning, but they know they are not to touch any of the objects—not that they would want to. Most of the people we've hired over the years tend to be much more superstitious about our collection than we are, and they refuse to touch anything strange or unusual, which is basically everything. Still, things get moved around from time to time, and I confronted the cleaner about the ventriloquist dolls.

"Did you move these?" I asked.

She looked at me like she'd rather stick her head in an oven than handle the Charlie McCarthy dolls.

The next time it happened, I found one of the dolls on the floor. It looked like he'd tried to climb down off the chair and landed in a heap.

It's an accident, I thought. *Someone bumped into the chair, or a gust of wind came in through the window. Nothing to be worried about.*

Then it happened again. This time, one of the dolls made it out of the library and into the hallway, where I found it on the floor near the stairs to the ground floor.

Was he trying to make a run for it? Where did he think he was going?

After that, I confronted Regina again. If she was messing with me, I needed to know.

"Seriously, Regina, did you move my dolls?"

"I swear on my father's grave I didn't."

For whatever reason, these dolls are a little out of the ordinary. Perhaps I absentmindedly picked them up and moved them around when I was really stressed out about something. I don't think I would ever do that—Regina would never let me hear the end of it if she caught me "playing with my dolls"—but it's a more likely explanation than the dolls suddenly being able to move around under their own power.

There was another incident, but I'm reluctant to mention it because I had consumed about half a bottle of wine when it happened. I went into the library to look for a book after dinner, and I swear I saw out of the corner of my eye one of the dolls blink on its own!

I've heard stories from other collectors who purchase objects that they believe have bad energy attached to them. My friend Guillermo del Toro, the famous movie director, had a mummy hand in his personal collection that he was convinced had negative powers. He got really weirded out about it and gave it back to the seller. I don't know if he even asked for a refund. He just wanted it gone.

I can't say that I've ever owned an object I felt was cursed, like that episode of *The Brady Bunch* where Greg finds a cursed idol and wears it around his neck for good luck, not realizing it's having the opposite effect. The only time I felt that something had negative energy attached to it was when I found out it was stolen. When I know something was improperly obtained, I no longer have any interest in keeping it. That's bad news as far as I'm concerned. That's the only time I'm like, "Get this fucking thing out of the house."

I am not terribly superstitious. I've certainly looked at objects I thought were kind of gross, but that's a matter of not liking the aesthetics of it. I would never assume something was inherently evil or bad.

The Charlie McCarthy dolls don't bother me. They don't give off a sinister vibe or anything like that. My feelings for them might change if I were to wake up one day to find one of the dolls sitting in my room or lying next to me in bed, staring at me with its unblinking doll eyes. That would definitely creep me out. And if they ever start talking, it's all over.

It wasn't until the dolls started to move around that I remembered the message the original collector had passed on to the dealer I bought them from, that these little guys needed a place where they could thrive, with space to move around. I hope they feel at home in our house.

I've come to accept that there's something different about these dolls. Of all the objects I own, they're the only pieces that have given me any kind of strange sensations. Just to be on the safe side, they now sit on the mantel alongside several artist dolls. If they're going to keep moving around, it's a long way to the floor, and they'll be taking some of their friends with them.

Do I think they're haunted?

Quite possibly.

———— •••• ————

THE EYE
Regina

I have a ghost story.

It happened not that long ago, right here in our home in Connecticut, which we moved into in 2020. We live in a beautiful, quaint New England village with a lot of very expensive old homes that are well taken care of. With Ryan's tailored suits, my high-fashion vampire look, and all of our tattoos, we don't look like we belong here. We're like the Addams family with the creepy house on the hill in an otherwise affluent and preppy town. I assume that's how people think of us here: the weird-looking couple with the house full of weird stuff.

The funny thing is that we may look weird to outsiders, but we're actually very polite and professional in everything we do, which surprises some people. I often wonder if they think we howl at the moon at night and sleep in coffins all day.

I don't want to say I'm cynical, but when it comes to ghosts, I never thought I'd see one. It wasn't something I sought out or was interested in. I wasn't a Goth kid, I don't particularly like scary movies, and before I met Ryan I didn't have any attachment to the macabre. I liked pretty clothes and Barbie dolls—but not so I could take them apart.

As a result of my Catholic upbringing, I've been exposed to a lot of morbid stuff—I just didn't see it that way at the time. When I started traveling around Europe with Ryan and looking at all this Catholic iconography and seeing images of martyred saints with their heads cut off or bleeding from their wounds, I thought, *This is really dark!* As I matured into adulthood, I started to notice that many of these icons were held up as examples of people who'd made the ultimate sacrifice for their faith.

That said, I'm way more morbid than Ryan. He's actually pretty upbeat. He's friendly and talkative and has an exuberant personality. He's pretty much in a good mood every single day from the moment he wakes up.

Not me. I'm much more like my mother, who is now in her late eighties. She has always been the most morbid person I know. When I was a young girl, she would say the most horrifying things to me at bedtime: "Come here and give me a kiss. I might be dead in the morning."

She talked about dying almost every single day of her life. To spend time with my mother is to receive a constant reminder that death is waiting for us all.

"This is why you're gonna live so long," I used to say to her, "because every time you say you're gonna die, God tacks on a couple more months."

I was only kidding then, but now I think it's true.

Unfortunately, I'm really morbid too. I have catastrophic thoughts. For example, if my dog sitter is five minutes late, I think some horrible accident has occurred and my dogs have suffered a tragic death. It's terrible. I am the most morbid thinker on the planet. My head goes to the darkest places, and I have my upbringing to thank for that.

Because of the way I grew up, I didn't know I was morbid, and I didn't know I had an interest in "the odd" until after I met Ryan. We've been to plenty of unusual places and handled lots of unusual stuff. And sometimes we brought those things home with us: straight-jackets and haunted mirrors and paintings that look like they were inspired by nightmares. Yet nothing out of the ordinary ever happened.

Until one day it did.

To be honest, I'm still a little freaked out by it.

Here's the story. I was upstairs in my changing room. I have a little boudoir where I get dressed and put on makeup. Everything is pink and quite feminine. My wardrobe is hidden, so when you come to the room, you are surrounded by artwork, taxidermy, and other ephemera that's all pink. It's the only room like this in the entire house.

One of those objects is a hand fashioned out of wax, and in the middle of its palm is a glass prosthetic eye. The preparation sits under a glass dome. This piece was purchased from Marina Gibbons, an artist we work with. It's very well made and not something I would think of as creepy, even though both the hand and the eye are lifelike.

The artist is an incredible sculptor who makes beautiful pieces with exceptional skill, which is something that sets her work apart. A great work of art should be a little mysterious. You shouldn't be able to figure out how it was made just by looking at it.

Marina exhibited her work at one of our events in Los Angeles. We'd never worked with her before, but we loved her sculptures and were excited that she was vending at our event. Ryan went to check out her booth, and when he came back, he told me that he thought she was pricing her work too low.

"People come here to spend money," he told her. "You're selling yourself short."

She was reluctant to raise her prices, so Ryan made her an offer she couldn't refuse.

"Raise your prices, and if your stuff doesn't sell, I'll buy it!"

She followed his advice, and sure enough Ryan had to eat his words. He ended up buying the most expensive piece she had, which was the wax hand with the glass eye. She shipped it to us from LA, and when it arrived I put it on a dresser in my boudoir where I keep a few other pieces.

Clockwise from top left

Nineteenth-century wax and bone anatomical preparation by Tramond of Paris. These models were originally used by medical professionals to demonstrate the relationship between the nerves, veins, and arteries and the cranium.

An early sample of a set of prosthetic legs for a child from the collection of Nick Parmesan. These were originally used by traveling salesmen to showcase the different models their company offered. These were popular during outbreaks of rickets and polio.

A very fine Victorian hand strengthener used to help exercise hands that had been injured or ravaged by arthritis

Rare, double-sided oil painting entitled *Portrait of a Man/Skull in a Niche* from 1535–55, by Barthel Bruyen the Elder from the collection of Richard Harris

Original drawing entitled *Two Skulls* by Julian Adolphe Duvocelle from 1898 from the collection of Richard Harris

Italian marble vanitas bust from the seventeenth century from the collection of Richard Harris

Mors Omnia Rapit (Death Ravages All) by Ryan Michael Cohn. It was created from a seventeenth-century Spanish wood santos bust with an embedded medical skull sealed in wax. The mask still retains its original glass eyes. The stand is made from hand-forged brass and mounted to a nineteenth-century marble plinth.

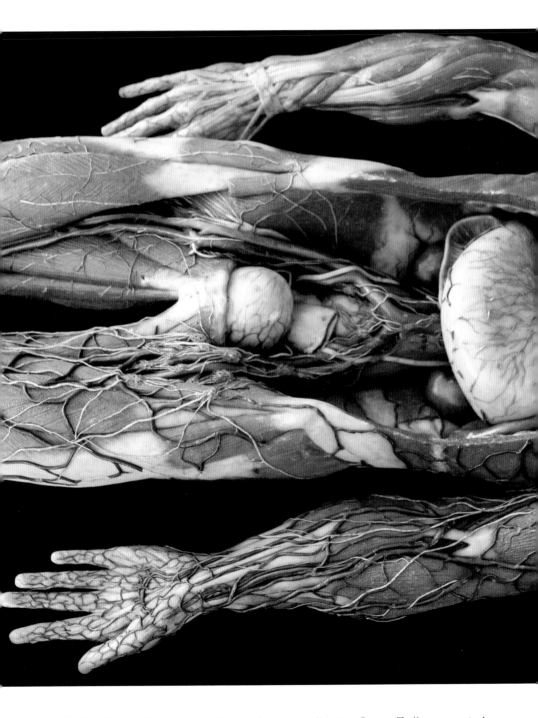

Definitely one of our favorite pieces in the entire collection. Gustav Zeiller anatomical écorché wax figure, which now resides at the Quttainah Historical Medical Museum in Kuwait.

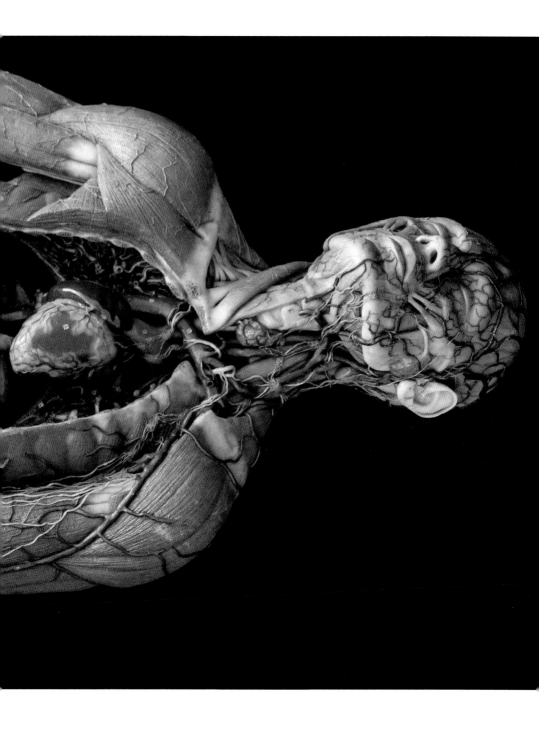

A pair of gilded eighteenth-century putti statues made of wood and polychrome with grotesque faces on their bellies

An original copy of *Thesaurus Animalism Primus* by Dutch anatomist Frederick Ruysch from 1710

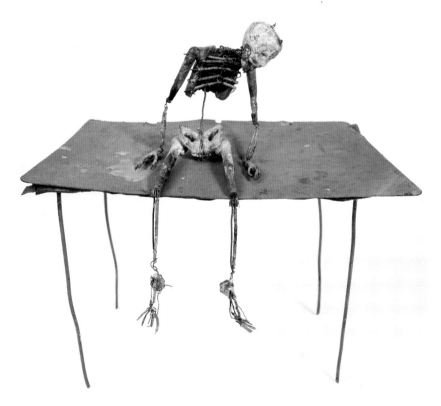

Mixed media work by artist June Leaf entitled "Gentleman on Green Table" from the collection of Richard Harris

Death of Venus by Roger Reutimann

One evening, I was in my boudoir getting dressed for a night out. Separating the boudoir from the primary bedroom is an Italian Renaissance–style room divider that's low enough that Ryan can peek over if he needs to speak with me, and vice versa. I was struggling with the zipper on my dress, which I couldn't quite reach, when all of a sudden I felt a hand assist me in zipping up my dress.

"Aw, thank you," I said. "That's so sweet."

Naturally, I thought it was Ryan who was helping me. It was especially thoughtful because I didn't have to ask for his help. He saw me struggling and came over to assist.

But when I turned around, Ryan wasn't there. There was nobody in the room with me—except for the hand, which was looking directly at me.

"Uh, Ryan?" I asked, but there was no answer.

"Ryan!" I yelled in a much louder voice.

"What?" Ryan answered from downstairs.

"Were you just upstairs?" I shouted, even though I knew the answer. "Were you in the room? Where you anywhere upstairs?"

"What are you talking about?" he said in that annoyed tone that husbands get when they think they're in trouble and don't know why.

"You have got to be kidding me!"

That's when I started to freak out, because not only did I feel a hand tugging on the zipper, but when I turned around, the only thing behind me was the hand—and it was literally looking right at me.

To say I was confused and utterly disturbed is an understatement.

It's not like the zipper magically zipped up on its own. That's not what happened, but I'm positive I felt someone or something tugging on it, like it was trying to help me. I felt it. As far as I'm concerned, that's an undeniable fact.

The hand doesn't give me a negative feeling. Quite the opposite. If I was indeed visited by some kind of spirit or supernatural entity or something beyond our ability to describe with words, it was a gentle, helpful presence.

Ryan, of course, is very protective of me. He asked if I wanted to sell the hand, and I told him I wasn't sure. I don't know if the house or the hand was responsible for assisting me with the dress, and not knowing is an unsettling feeling.

Nothing's happened since. I still have the hand in my boudoir, but I'm kind of afraid to touch it. Every time I walk by it, I wonder if I'll ever feel something like that again.

THE CREEPY COFFINS
Ryan & Regina

Sometimes we get offers to buy things that are just too creepy—even for us. This is a story about one of those times. It's also a story about how a deal can fall apart at the last minute.

We were in Rhode Island visiting Regina's mother when we received an offer to buy a Victorian coffin called the Fisk Metallic Burial Case. These were airtight, cast-iron coffins with a glass front so you could see the face of the person entombed inside. They were beautifully made and very expensive for their time.

When someone died in the mid-nineteenth century, you couldn't put the body on a plane to ship it home or hop in a car to attend the funeral service. Some time might elapse between death and burial, and the benefits of an airtight coffin that preserved the body and didn't leak or smell were very attractive to those who could afford the expense. The Fisk burial cases were also aesthetically pleasing, resembling an Egyptian sarcophagus. President Zachary Taylor was buried in a Fisk coffin.

We were intrigued by the offer. Although Fisk made quite a few of these coffins in a range of sizes, they're incredibly rare today because the people who bought them tended to use them. You typically only see them in funerary museums. Sometimes a small town museum will have one in its collection, but they hardly ever come up for sale. A cool coincidence was that we got the offer while we were in Rhode Island—the place where the coffins were originally manufactured by Almond Dunbar Fisk.

The email came from a woman in the Midwest. We'll call her Carla Coffin. She said she had five burial cases for sale. We'd only seen one of these before. For someone to have five was just unheard of.

"We're interested in all of them," we wrote. "What's your price?

Carla wrote back right away. "Oh, gee, I don't know. I haven't really thought about it."

This happens a lot. Sometimes a seller will try to gauge the interest in a piece before they settle on a price.

"First things first," we said. "You need to figure out what you want, because we don't want just one. We want them all."

"Well, actually," Carla responded, "we were thinking about keeping the baby one."

With infant mortality rates so high in the nineteenth century, Fisk manufactured a coffin for very small children, but they didn't make many of them. The child's coffin was the one we wanted the most.

We wrote back and told her it was basically all or nothing. Carla agreed and called us on the phone to discuss the terms.

"We'd like $12,000 for all five of them," she said.

That seemed fair enough. If the coffins were in good condition, we could get about $5,000 for each one. We figured after transportation, shipping, and the time involved in reselling them, we'd keep the infant coffin and turn a profit.

As we continued the conversation we started to ask more questions about where the coffins were located and what kind of condition they were in. We learned that Carla had an Instagram page that advertised all kinds of coffins for sale, including the Fisk Metallic Burial Cases, that was getting lots of attention from collectors. It was time to make the deal happen and I was ready to send a check.

But first we needed to know a bit more information, namely where did these coffins come from? These cases clearly didn't come from Goodwill or someone's basement. Carla seemed to have a side hustle selling coffins, but where was she getting them?

"Well," she said, "my husband is a gravedigger."

That was a huge red flag, but it wasn't necessarily a deal-breaker. If her husband was indeed a professional gravedigger, he might have legitimate access to a funeral home that was going out of business. Obviously, we needed more information.

"Where did these coffins come from?" we asked point-blank.

Carla's response was convoluted. Her story just didn't add up. She told us that a friend was clearing a large piece of property, and that's where the coffins came from.

That wasn't going to cut it. We needed more details. What did she mean? Had these coffins been dug up?

The next time we talked on the phone, Carla said something very strange.

"I just spoke to my husband. I don't think we can sell you the child's coffin, and I can't tell you why."

"Why can't you tell us?" we asked.

We told her that we weren't going to buy *any* of the coffins if there was any weirdness attached to them. We explained that we're well-known collectors and that everything we do is aboveboard. If Carla couldn't prove that she owned these coffins, we weren't interested.

The longer we talked, the stranger her story became. Carla and her husband were involved in the sale of a piece of land, and they were tasked with excavating the property where several people had been buried. She claimed that the remains had been disinterred long ago, but the coffins were still in the ground.

"Thanks, but no thanks," we said, and that was the end of that.

The sad thing is that while we passed on that deal, some collectors will jump on an opportunity like that because they don't have much of a moral compass. We get offers like this with such frequency that we've become very good at sniffing out the bad ones. For us, if it doesn't feel right, it probably isn't.

ANATOMY LESSONS

This photo of Princess Andromeda has appeared on numerous taxidermy blogs and websites, which have assumed she's a poorly crafted piece of taxidermy. Andromeda, however, is alive and doing very well! Note: She still climbs atop this massive hippo skull to get away from the three dogs.

THE ART OF WAX
Ryan

O ne of the reasons I pursued the Max Wax deal so diligently was that I didn't have any stellar wax pieces in my collection, but it wasn't for lack of trying.

The first wax model I ever purchased was a nineteenth-century mannequin head. During the late nineteenth century and into the early part of the twentieth century, wax heads and mannequins were used for displays in department stores, tailor shops, and other places where clothing was modeled and sold. Retailers would put real hair on them and even used glass eyes and porcelain skulls that looked astonishingly real. Today, most mannequins are made of fiberglass, plastic, or other materials.

I was on the hunt for a wax mannequin head for a long time before I finally found one in good condition. A complete wax mannequin was impossible to find; they tended to break or have damage from improper storage. They weren't thought of as art and thus weren't treated as such. They were commercial objects. If a mannequin was badly damaged, it would be salvaged for parts—first by business owners and then by collectors.

I found a number of different wax mannequin heads over the years, and I was constantly upgrading them. I liked having one or two in my collection because they looked cool alongside other examples of all the ways the human face could be presented. I would display the mannequin with my jewelry or with different kinds of medical apparatuses.

To be honest, the mannequin heads didn't really satisfy my desire for wax sculptures. What I really wanted was an anatomical wax model, which was even harder to find. To understand why I wanted one of these waxworks so badly, you have to understand the history of wax sculpting.

Wax figures have been used to titillate and terrify, but they also played a critical role in medical and scientific communities. It's no secret that early anatomists and surgeons relied on human cadavers to better understand the body's complex systems. Because these cadavers were only viable for a short period of time, there was always a shortage, and unscrupulous doctors resorted to all manner of unsavory tactics, from robbing graves to procuring fresh corpses from hospitals without proper consent.

The first anatomical waxwork was believed to have been created in the seventeenth century by Italian sculptor Gaetano Zumbo with assistance from French surgeon Guillaume Desnoues. As early as 1665, a Dutch anatomist named Frederik Ruysch was experimenting with embalming techniques by injecting melted wax into a cadaver's blood vessels. The wax was mixed with a special dye that he kept a closely guarded secret. The red mixture, visible just below the surface of the skin, lent a rosy glow to his dissections, which he placed in jars of alcohol for preservation. Once this process was completed, Ruysch arranged his preparations in lifelike poses; this made them more aesthetically appealing and also served as a commentary on the fleeting nature of life.

One of Ruysch's most famous preparations shows a collection of fetal skeletons arranged around a pile of gallstones and preserved organs. The central figure "plays" a violin with a bow made out of a dried artery. Many of Ruysch's preparations took on a moral tone. He often decorated amputated limbs and severed heads with lace cuffs and collars to make them appear more lifelike. Ruysch believed the intricacies of embroidered lace mirrored the inner workings of the body.

During his lifetime, Ruysch produced over two thousand preparations that he collected in five rooms of his home and showed off to his peers, students, and guests. He wrote detailed catalogs, which he furnished with elaborate illustrations. The famed anatomist lived to be ninety-three, and toward the end of his life, he sold off his entire collection to Russian czar Peter the Great.

Ruysch's techniques inspired anatomists around the world who helped solve the troubling problem of procuring fresh corpses for medical students. Why not create realistic wax models of the human body that would not deteriorate and could be used over and over again?

Michel De Spiegelaere's *Scene Macabre* made of resin skeletons and mixed media. An ode to Dutch anatomist Frederik Ruysch.

Wax is mutable and durable. It could be used to express the minute specificity of the body and convey a range of emotions as wide as the human experience. However, making such intricate models required a very unique skill set: an intimate understanding of the workings of human anatomy and the artistry to recreate those details in wax.

Enter Gustav Zeiller, his brother Paul Zeiller, Adolf Ziegler, and E. E. Hammer, to name just a few. These are some of the greatest artists of the nineteenth century, but most people don't know their names because of the stigma attached to the medium in which they worked: wax.

These artists were masters at dissection and écorché (a figure sculpted to show the muscles and bones of the body). The wax models they created were used to show the skeletal system, the muscular system, the arterial system, and so on. Their waxworks were often enlarged because they were used in anatomical amphitheaters so that students could see the presentation from a distance. The work of these artist-anatomists was exceptionally vivid and striking because the figures were literally larger than life. Thanks to their efforts, medical professionals and students alike could learn not only how the intricate systems of the human body worked but also how they were interconnected to create the miracle of life.

It's helpful to remember that the realms of art and science were not as distinct then as they are today. Many early practitioners in these fields saw them as flip sides of the same coin. Both artists and anatomists had a professional interest in studying the intricacies of the human form, and both wanted to unravel the mystery of what animates these interconnected systems of tissue, muscle, and bone. Ruysch, for example, illustrated his anatomy books with figures of fetal skeletons in whimsical poses. What might seem grisly in another context made his work more aesthetically pleasing to his readers—most of whom were not medical professionals.

This exchange of ideas between artists and anatomists went both ways. For *The Raft of the Medusa*, French artist Théodore Géricault used actual cadavers as models for the dead and dying sailors awaiting rescue during an ill-fated voyage on the perilous raft. While he was painting this masterpiece in the early 1820s, Géricault's studio resembled an anatomist's laboratory with the discarded body parts that he used in his studies.

For me, the anatomical models created by Zeiller, Ziegler, Hammer, and others were giant, three-dimensional versions of the images I used to copy out of my parents' encyclopedia. I longed to get my hands on one of those beauties, but the chances of stumbling upon a wax sculpture by Gustav Zeiller in a Brooklyn flea market were slim to none. The items were just too rare. Because they were predominantly created in Europe, anatomical wax models were hardly ever made available for sale in the United States.

Prior to purchasing the Max Wax collection, the finest wax specimens I owned were a series of scientific models produced by the Ziegler studio for the classroom. After Adolf Ziegler died in 1889, his son Friedrich took over the business. In 1892, the studio produced a series displaying the development of a frog from an embryo to a tadpole to a mature specimen. I've bought and sold a few of those sets over the years. They were fascinating to look at, but a tadpole doesn't have the same impact as a life-size anatomical model of the human body.

When the opportunity to acquire the Max Wax collection presented itself, I was ecstatic. It was easily the most incredible collection of anatomical models I had ever seen, and I wanted to keep some of the pieces for our own collection. When all was said and done, we held on to approximately twenty moulages, including three astonishing sculptures by Gustav Zeiller, the Leonardo da Vinci of anatomical modeling.

Two of the Zeiller works are oversize busts of the human head with the skin peeled back to reveal layers of muscle as well as the vascular, circulatory, and nervous systems. These would have been used in an amphitheater for medical students learning about the inner workings of the face and head. They were made on a larger scale so that everyone in the room could properly see the models.

You might think that presenting a human likeness in this manner would be horrifying, like having a larger-than-life model of a Cenobite from *Hellraiser* in your home. Zeiller was so talented, meticulous, and gifted that he was able to subtly imbue his models with emotions—the essence of humanity. They are more than anatomical models; they are meditations on the marvels of the human body that we all too often take for granted.

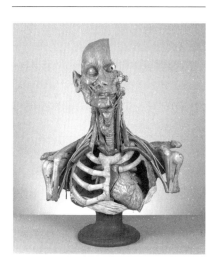

Oversized anatomical wax écorché bust by anatomist and artist Gustav Zeiller from the mid-nineteenth century. This wax moulage was once used to teach medical students in an anatomical theater. The model was made on a larger scale to enable students seated farther away to properly see the preparation.

The third écorché model by Zeiller was an oversize representation of a complete human figure. It was an astonishingly lifelike piece, but we had to let it go. The massive model lay prone like a corpse on an embalming table. It was stamped with numbers that would have corresponded with the curriculum for teaching a course in anatomy. Perhaps even more remarkably, it was signed by the artist himself. It truly was an incredible piece, and with its large size and exposed anatomy, it looked a bit like Dr. Frankenstein's monster. It sometimes seemed like all the wax model needed was a jolt of electricity to shock it to life.

The model was so remarkable that we felt we had to sell it. That may sound counterintuitive, but while we owned the piece it suffered a minor mishap. It was too big for any of the living spaces in our home—it would take up an entire room—so we had it down in the basement, which is also my workspace.

Compared to the storage spaces we were used to in the city, our basement is a vast labyrinthine chamber that runs the entire length of the house. It's where we store the hundreds of pieces that aren't quite ready to be displayed. However, compared to Max Wax's subterranean storage area in Munich, our basement is not all that different from the unfinished basements you find in old homes throughout the northeast. It's a dark, claustrophobic place packed with oddities and antiques and filled with nooks and alleyways. It's easy to stub your toe or hit your head on the pipes that snake through the exposed ceiling. It reminds me of being on a ship. It's wild down there. A little dangerous, a little creepy—especially if you don't know your way around.

While I was working on a cabinet for another piece, a glass door broke and rained shattered glass all over the Zeiller waxwork. The model required a minor restoration that involved painstakingly removing all the bits of glass. After that, I was afraid something truly calamitous would happen to Zeiller's masterpiece. We didn't have it on display, so we weren't really enjoying the piece like we do with most of the items in our collection.

Although the sculpture worked well with the rest of our pieces, it needed a proper, museum-quality cabinet. However, this would require a lot of work to build and would be very costly. Then the piece would take up even more space, and we'd have to clear out several other objects in our collection to make room for it. I was starting to get the feeling that we might not be able to put it on display in our house and that we lacked the resources to accommodate the piece. It was just too big.

We were on the fence about what to do with it when a storm swept through the Connecticut coast, flooding our basement. When we moved into our house, all the neighbors told us, "I've lived here for forty years, and I've never had water in my basement."

During the storm, just about everyone in the area had flooding in their basements. It was a crazy scene. We came down the stairs and there was water covering the entire floor of the basement. I had three sump pumps down there, but the problem was that water has to reach a certain level before they start working. If there's half an inch of water everywhere, the pumps won't turn on, which wasn't ideal. We were trying to get rid of the water that was already in the basement, not wait until the problem got worse.

None of the pieces we had down there—including the Zeiller—were damaged, but I lost a lot of my drawings as well as some artwork. A few framed items leaning against the walls got wet. Artwork that's been water damaged is very difficult to restore because the water warps the paper and leaves a stain. We had to elevate everything off the ground and thoroughly ventilate the place for weeks afterward to make sure we didn't have any mold issues down there.

After the storm passed, I started to lose sleep over the waxwork in the basement. The longer I left the piece downstairs, the greater the likelihood that something terrible was going to happen to it. The flood was a wake-up call. I realized it was no longer worth the worry that came with keeping such a valuable work in my basement. Frankly, the piece deserved better.

Even though it was one of my favorites, I eventually felt good about parting with it. When you really love something, it takes a lot to get to that point. I had to look at the big picture and recognize that I wanted what was best for the piece. I was finally able to accept that sitting in our basement wasn't an ideal situation for an extremely rare and sensitive waxwork sculpture. That's when I knew it was time to put this magnificent work of art into someone else's collection.

I always told myself that if we ever sold the piece, it would have to go to a proper collection. I didn't want to sell it to just anybody. I reached out to my old friend Guillermo del Toro, who had asked me to contact him if I was ever interested in selling any of the individual pieces of the Max Wax collection.

He recognized the extraordinary nature of the Zeiller waxwork but decided it wasn't a good time for such a large anatomical wax sculpture. "As much as I want to buy this," he told us, "I just don't want to add anything of substantial size right now."

That was disappointing, but I had a short list of private collectors who had expressed interest in the piece in the past. Unfortunately, the timing wasn't right, and they all passed.

One of our favorite pieces being crated and shipped to its new home in Kuwait! A very special crate had to be custom-fashioned for this extremely fragile and valuable anatomical model.

Next, we considered finding a home for it at a museum, which was challenging. The price of the piece was prohibitive for many institutions. Highly specialized museums generally don't have the kind of money it takes to acquire a piece like this.

We ended up selling the Zeiller waxwork to a historical medical museum in Kuwait that other collectors we know have sold anatomical curiosities to. We felt good knowing it would be taken care of by a team of professional curators and displayed in a way that it could be enjoyed by the public. If we ever want to see Zeiller's sculpture again, we can hop on a plane and pay it a visit.

We don't own any models by Gustav's brother Paul, but we do have a nineteenth-century book he wrote about human anatomy. I bought it in the hopes of finding out more about the pieces we'd acquired, perhaps seeing a diagram or a photograph, but also to learn more about these talented and trailblazing brothers whose alternative to dissecting the corpses of the destitute was met with such opposition in Munich scientific circles.

Plus, it's always a good thing if you can document the items in your collection with secondary sources. Ultimately, it increases the value of the piece because it tells potential buyers that it has cultural and/or historical significance beyond one's appreciation of its beauty.

At this point in our lives, we'd like to keep only the very best wax models, but we're always careful about selling items from the Max Wax collection because they mean so much to us—both as collectors and as a couple.

AMISH ADVENTURES
Ryan & Regina

After we bought the Max Wax collection, we started to get offers from other collectors who were sitting on wax models they wanted to sell. A typical email would sound like this:

"Greetings! I have twenty busts from a wax museum. Are you interested?"

You better believe it!

In fact, we strongly considered buying the anatomical models from a torture museum in Belgium. These museums typically display medieval instruments of torture and occasionally use wax figures to demonstrate how the devices worked. Because the moulages resembled the pieces in Max Wax's collection, we wondered if they'd been acquired from Castan's Panopticum.

We wanted to find out, especially since the collection included a couple of animatronic pieces, or automatons. It turns out our suspicions were correct—the models were indeed produced by modelers working for Castan's Panopticum, but the problem was the asking price. The sellers wanted a ridiculous amount of money for the collection. In addition, it was going to cost a small fortune to ship it overseas. After the mysterious fees that were tacked on to the Max Wax collection, we were reluctant to take on that kind of risk. We took all of those factors into consideration and submitted a counteroffer, but by that time, the collection had been sold. You can't win them all.

Although we didn't have much luck overseas, we again partnered up with our friend Tim League from the Alamo Drafthouse Cinema to procure a collection much closer to home: an Amish wax museum in Pennsylvania. A one-room schoolhouse from 1870 had been turned into a museum and furnished with animatronic wax figures that recreated scenes from Amish school life. The intent was wholesome, but many of the wax figures had deteriorated over the years, and the overall effect was incredibly creepy.

Someone from the museum posted an ad on Craigslist, and that's how we found out about the collection. Everyone kept tagging us on social media, and by the time we saw it, Tim League was already reaching out to us.

"Let's go get this thing," Tim said. "Maybe we can open another bar!"

An Amish-themed bar?

Why not!

We talked about designing another bar with the Alamo Drafthouse Cinema. After we drove to Pennsylvania and secured the collection, we flew out to Los Angeles with the construction team

from House of Wax to scope out a property. Naturally, everyone thought we were crazy.

"You want to open an Amish-themed bar? In Los Angeles?"

Ultimately, the skepticism was warranted. The collection didn't make sense for the space.

Not long after that, we procured another collection for Tim. This collection was also in Pennsylvania and, believe it or not, was from an Amish amusement park that doubled as a petting zoo. The wax figures Tim wanted were arranged in a stirring barn-raising scene. Again, we didn't actually buy the pieces. We just drove down to the Keystone State to pick them up for Tim. It's weird out there in Amish country, and they probably thought the same thing about us.

Wax animatronic Amish figure collection from Pennsylvania's oldest one-room school house!

Both collections of Amish waxworks are currently in a temperature-controlled storage unit in Texas, waiting to be unleashed on an unsuspecting public.

MONKEY BUSINESS
Regina

I n our line of work, you often have to be quick, but sometimes you have to be patient and play the long game. Ryan happens to excel at both of these aspects. I've seen him spend months and months researching an object while we wait for the right circumstances to fall into place. In fact, Ryan once waited over twenty years to get what he wanted. He got it in the end, but as the saying goes, be careful what you wish for.

Early in our relationship, Ryan took me on a trip to Hudson, New York. Hudson is a bucolic little town on the east side of the Hudson River about 120 miles from New York City. Even though only a few thousand people live there, it's filled with a plethora of antique stores and old Victorian homes. It's one of the few towns in the northeast that is still like that. We love it there. When we go on buying trips to Hudson, we'll make a weekend of it and spend a few days in town. It's actually one of the places we considered moving to when we were thinking about leaving the city and buying a house. It's not that far from NYC, but it's really small. Head a few blocks in any direction and you're surrounded by fields. It's a whole other world up there, which many people discovered when they moved from the city to Hudson during the pandemic.

Ryan explained to me that when he was fifteen years old, his parents took him to a particular antique store in Hudson. The shop wasn't dedicated to oddities or anything like that. It was just your typical fancy antique store that has been around forever. What made it unique for Ryan was that the store had a taxidermied monkey that sat on top of a cabinet near the entrance as if to greet everyone who came into the store. Ryan was completely captivated by it. He thought it was the coolest thing in the world.

"Is the monkey for sale?" he asked the man behind the counter.

"Nope," he said, "that's our mascot."

As Ryan became interested in collecting oddities, and as his reputation grew, he never forgot about that monkey and kept going back to Hudson. Every time he visited the shop, he would ask about it, but the answer was always the same: not for sale.

Ryan explained all this to me as we made our way to the store. When we got there, it was closed. We stood outside and looked through the window.

"This is the store I was telling you about," Ryan explained, "where this asshole won't sell me his monkey."

What Ryan didn't realize was that the owner was standing right behind us, talking to one of his neighbors, and he heard everything Ryan said.

Ryan tried to downplay the situation—"Oh, hey, how's it going?"—but he was so embarrassed. Ryan was on good terms with the owner and had bought some things from him over the years, but he really wanted that monkey. After all those years, he was still obsessed with it, which I thought was hilarious. At that point in his career, the monkey would no longer be a standout addition to his collection. I didn't think it was all that remarkable, to tell you the truth. But for Ryan, it was a battle of wills. He had to have the monkey.

A few years later, around the time that we bought our house in Connecticut, we paid another visit to Hudson. We weren't there on a buying trip. We had just bought the house and needed to be frugal with our finances, but we found some incredible pieces at some of the other stores in town. The first piece was a huge, eighteenth-century, hand-painted Spanish carving of Jesus on the cross. The second was an incredibly ornate cast-iron daybed that belonged to Andy Warhol. Cherubs and flowers adorn the bed, which has a beautiful patina showing its age. Warhol had an estate in the Hamptons that

SPECIMENS FROM OUR TAXIDERMY COLLECTION

- *Monkey head with a crown of thorns*
- *Three Indian peacocks*
- *Miniature Victorian puppy*
- *Mr. Peepers*
- *Pair of swans*

was filled with Victorian furniture, including this antique daybed. It was extremely expensive, but we bought it anyway. Both pieces are now part of our personal collection.

Even though we had already spent more money than we were supposed to, Ryan wanted to go check on the monkey.

"Hey, are you ready to sell that monkey?" he asked.

The guy smiled and shook his head. "Sorry, we don't want to sell him, but you'll be the first to know if he ever goes up for sale."

A few months passed, and then something really tragic happened. Ryan got a text from the owner of the store: "We have some sad news, but maybe good news for you. We're finally ready to part with the monkey, but he's not in good shape."

Ryan called the owner of the store and found out there had been a horrible flood. The water spilled into his store from a cracked pipe in the ceiling and destroyed 70 percent of the antiques in the shop, including the monkey. It was just a devastating situation, and now the owner wanted to get rid of the monkey.

"You can have him," the owner said, "but I'll warn you. It's a pretty grisly sight."

An example of what can go terribly wrong with a piece of taxidermy. Mr. Peepers in his final stages of life.

So we drove all the way up to Hudson, which is about two hours away. Sure enough, the monkey was in bad shape. It had sustained water damage in the flood, and most of the fur had slipped off the form. There were still bits of fur sticking up here and there, which was really weird looking. To be honest, it looked like something out of a nightmare.

Did Ryan still want it?

Of course he did.

We bought a few other things that were in decent condition to help the owner out, and brought the monkey home. For some odd reason, Ryan decided to call him Mr. Peepers. For the most part, we don't give names to the objects in our collection. If we were to give every item in our collection a name, I think I'd end up needing professional help.

Unfortunately, Mr. Peepers is still sitting in a box down in the basement. I don't think it can be saved, otherwise Ryan would have done something with it by now.

For us, it's a reminder of the devastating effects of Mother Nature. Whether it's a flood or a fire or some other natural disaster, you can pay a terrible price when you hang on to something too long.

———— •••• ————

SAM SHARP
Ryan

I knew a guy in Williamsburg, Brooklyn, who worked at an antique store in town. Let's call him Sam Sharp.

Sam was very friendly, and we had a good relationship dating back to when I was working out of Against Nature. I made some custom jewelry for him—a ring that he designed—but there were some delays because I was so busy at the time. He got pretty pissed off about how long it was taking and yelled at me. When I finished the ring, he was really happy with it and apologized for his outburst. He gave me a bottle of whiskey, and we became friendly again.

I didn't see Sam for a little while until he started working at an antique store in Williamsburg that I would visit from time to time. We would just chat here and there when we saw each other at the store. One time, he mentioned that he was working for a private collector who was looking to move some things and that there were a few pieces that might be of interest to me. He was kind of vague about the details, but some people are like that. They want you to know they've got something special even if they aren't willing or able to share what it is.

He piqued my curiosity, and every few months I would reach out to him. He had mentioned there were multiple mummies and shrunken heads in the collection, which definitely got my attention. When it comes to collecting, I can be extremely patient. I can play the long game, but I'm also very persistent.

"Hey, man," I wrote, "I'd love to know what's in that collection."

He finally responded with a photo of a vintage set of gynecological instruments from Charrière of Paris, a French company that made medical equipment. In the nineteenth century, doctors mostly worked out of their patients' homes, so they needed to bring their own tools with them when they went on house calls. Charrière of Paris made sets of tools for every occasion: surgery, amputation, etc. This particular set was made for midwifery, or what we would call obstetrics today. The set came in a stylish-looking wooden case that made the instruments seem almost elegant, which was the point. You don't want your surgeon rolling up to your house looking like a carpenter or a handyman.

I already had a small collection of medical instruments, but it just so happened that my focus was on Charrière of Paris. This particular set was from around the 1880s, but it wasn't the best that I'd seen. It came in a wooden case with velvet lining. I wrote back and told him I was interested in purchasing it.

"I'm not quite ready to sell it," he said.

I thought this was odd since he was the one who'd sent me the details about the instruments. Sometimes people want to gauge interest in a piece before they sell it, or maybe he was being wishy-washy about the whole thing. Either way, I felt as though he was wasting my time.

"Sell it or don't, but when you make up your mind let me know."

About a year later, he got back to me. "I'm finally ready to part with that gynecological set," he wrote. "How much do you want to offer?"

My problem with the piece was that there was a strong possibility it had been infested with mites. The velvet had deteriorated slightly, and I could see what looked like tiny pinholes in the fabric. This is something that you have to be very, very mindful of when you're dealing with anything like books or textiles because you won't know the insects are there until it's too late. Once mites get into the fibers, they methodically do their thing until one day you go to open a book and discover it has turned to dust. The same thing with moths. You have to be very careful about this stuff.

We went back and forth, and I bought the set for $1,000, which was a fairly good deal. I figured a set like that was probably worth about $2,500 or maybe $3,500 at auction if it was cleaned up and restored. I think I got the piece for less than he wanted because of the possible mite issue, but you can never be too careful.

As soon as I obtained the set, I put it in the freezer to prevent any bugs that might be hiding inside from mating and to prevent future bugs from hatching. This also works with moths. If you suspect an item is infested with moths, simply put it in the freezer for a week or two, and that will typically kill off the adults and prevent them from breeding. If you want to prevent infestations, get a bug trap that uses pheromones as a lure. That will attract the males and kill them off before they breed, and eventually the females will die as well.

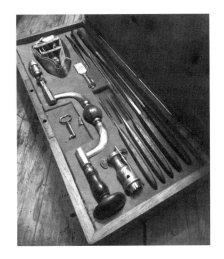

A rare cased trephination and amputation set once used by a field doctor to attend to the wounded during and after battle. These sets were also used by traveling surgeons for home visits.

However, there was one thing about the sale that I thought was strange. When Sam brought the gynecological set to my home and we completed the transaction, he said something I thought was unusual.

"Do me a favor and don't share the image on social media."

It's mine now, I thought to myself, *and I'll do whatever I want with it.*

We're high-profile collectors. Our collection is always being photographed or filmed. So there's a chance that even if I were to keep the image off of social media, it's just a matter of time before it shows up in the background of a photo spread or video. Also, I often put exhibitions together for museums and arts organizations. If I were to include the gynecological set someday, I'd have no control over who was photographing it and what they did with the images.

I was a little suspicious, but some sellers will try to put unrealistic stipulations on a piece. "I'll sell it to you," they might say, "but you can't resell it. This is for your collection and not anyone else's."

I never agree to these terms. If I buy it, I own it. That means I can do whatever I want with it. I think requests like these are a form of seller's remorse. They're happy to have the item off their hands, but they haven't gotten used to the idea of relinquishing control of the object. They still want to have some say in what happens to the piece even after they sell it. Sellers want their pieces to go to a good home—that's not unusual—but sometimes they're not ready to confront the reality that someone else might be able to profit from a piece they looked after for so long.

So I didn't think too much of Sam's comments. I knew from the start he was having a hard time letting go of the piece.

At least that's what I thought.

About a year later, I got a very unusual call. "Do you know Sam Sharp?" the official-sounding voice on the other end of the line asked.

"Yes. May I ask who's calling?"

"This is Agent So-and-So from the FBI. Can you tell us what you know about this individual?"

Once I got over my shock, I told the agent that he was a nice guy and that I'd purchased a few things from him over the years. "Is there a problem?" I asked.

"Well," the agent said, "he's been accused of stealing four hundred thousand dollars' worth of merchandise." It turns out that Sam was stealing items from the storage unit of the private collector that he was working for and then selling the stuff to other collectors and at flea markets.

"It looks like you purchased a vintage surgical set from Sam."

"Yes, I did," I said. "I bought it for one thousand dollars, but I had no idea that it was stolen. I'm happy to give it to you if you like so it can be returned to whomever it belongs to, but what about the thousand dollars I shelled out? What happens with that?"

"We're not sure if the instruments are stolen. We just know that he sold them to you."

"So what do I do now?" I asked.

"We'll be in touch."

Obviously, I was a little freaked out. I took the set off the shelf and packed it up so I could send it off to the FBI when they got back to me. As far as I was concerned, the set was tainted, and I didn't want it associated with my collection.

Days went by, and we didn't hear back from the agent, but we followed the case in the news. Eventually, Sam Sharp was convicted and went to jail, where he remains to this day. As for the stolen set of vintage gynecological instruments, we stashed them in a storage locker.

A few years later, I got an email from Sam, except it wasn't Sam. It was his girlfriend using his email. She said she had some stuff from Sam's collection, and she was trying to sell it.

"Are you interested?" she asked.

"No thanks," I said. "We're good."

We never did hear back from the FBI.

CHAPTER VIII

THE
NICK PARMESAN COLLECTION

DEATH OF A COLLECTOR

BEST CHICKEN PARM IN TOWN

CARROLL GARDENS

EXCAVATING THE COLLECTION

Photo of Nick Parmesan long before
we got to know him

DEATH OF A COLLECTOR
Ryan & Regina

A couple of years ago, we were having dinner in the city when we received a text with some sad news. Nick Parmesan, a friend and fellow collector whom we introduced at the beginning of the book, had just passed away from cancer. The news came as a shock because we didn't know he was sick. No one did. Nick hadn't even told his family about his diagnosis.

That part didn't surprise us. To be honest, nothing about Nick surprised us. He was a secretive guy with an extensive collection of oddities and unusual artifacts. He also had a *lot* of enemies.

Nick had a knack for rubbing people in the collecting community the wrong way. He drove a hard bargain, and he had a way of wearing people out when he was negotiating with them that didn't always go over well. Nick was a former sergeant in the New York Police Department, and at times he could be overly aggressive. When he really wanted something, he pulled out all the stops. He truly knew how to break people down, like an expert in interrogation, which was probably part of his previous career.

All collectors are a little strange. It's practically a prerequisite in this business, but Nick was unusual by any standard. He was tall, lanky, and a little emaciated-looking. He wore his hair in a stringy ponytail. He had the teeth of a lifelong smoker and was always sipping on a can of Monster Energy.

Although Nick was a little off, he was an exceptional collector. He may have been a hobbyist, but he had better instincts than many professional antiquarians we've known. To succeed in this business, you have to develop an instinct for identifying unique objects. Nick's sensibilities were borderline uncanny, like a sixth sense. Whatever you want to call that quality, Nick had it.

We weren't the closest of friends, and we had our ups and downs, which we'll get to in a little bit, but we liked Nick despite his rough edges. Few people would call him kind or gentle or caring, but we saw those qualities in him. Because he liked us, he let his guard down with us and showed a side of himself that others didn't get to see. We were sad to hear the news that he'd passed. We would miss him.

We were also going to miss that amazing chicken parm. Whenever Nick wanted something, he would try to butter us up by bringing over a tray of chicken parmesan from his family's deli. More often than not, the tactic worked.

After we were informed of Nick's passing, we reached out to his brother to give our condolences. We also wanted to share our concerns. Having been in this business for a while, we knew that unscrupulous collectors were going to try and take advantage of the situation by telling Nick's siblings that they were his best friend.

The sad truth was that Nick didn't have many friends. He had business relationships, and very few of those relationships ended well. Nick didn't really have tight bonds with people. In fact, a lot of people *hated* Nick because of how intense and unpleasant he could be during negotiations.

We'd seen it with our own eyes, and although we'd worked through our issues with Nick, most of the people he dealt with never gave him a second chance. They would have no qualms about taking advantage of Nick's loved ones while they were grieving. It was a terrible situation for the family.

Nick was full of secrets. Not only did he keep his poor health from his family, but they had no idea that his apartment was filled with rare, one-of-a-kind objects that were worth a considerable amount of money.

How much was his collection worth? No one really knew because no one knew what he had, but it was a lot. He had *thousands* of pieces in his collection, and it was all buried underneath mountains of junk. Nick's family didn't know about the garbage, either. They had no idea he was a hoarder.

On top of all that, his landlord wanted everything out of the apartment immediately so that they could renovate the place and rent it out as soon as possible. The apartment had been in the family and under rent control for something like fifty years. Nick's death meant the owners could finally raise the rent.

It was a lot for Nick's family to deal with, especially after Nick's sudden death. We told Nick's brother that if they needed to authenticate any of the pieces in Nick's collection or if they wanted to talk about any of the individual items, we'd be happy to help. We also made it clear that if they were thinking of selling the collection, they should definitely give us a call.

A few days later, we got a call from an antiques dealer in the neighborhood who warned us that another dealer was pressuring Nick's family to sell the collection. "You've got to call Nick's sister," she said, "otherwise this guy is going to get Nick's collection for a song."

We didn't want to see Nick's family taken advantage of by an unscrupulous dealer. We had to do something. But before we discuss what happened next, we need to go back to our earliest dealings with Nick.

—— ◆◆◆ ——

BEST CHICKEN PARM IN TOWN
Ryan

After *Oddities* was canceled, I went back to making my living by seeking out strange and unusual artifacts full-time. Sometimes that meant putting myself in strange and unusual situations.

Because of *Oddities*, I had a high profile as a collector, especially in New York. The first time I met Nick, he approached me at a flea market in Brooklyn that I happened to be selling at. I didn't know him, but I'd seen him around. He didn't have a shop or a gallery. He was one of the many oddballs in the collecting scene who was always lurking around antique shops, auction houses, and flea markets on the hunt for who knows what.

He was really polite and showed a lot of interest in the things I was selling that day. I had a skullcap filled with teeth that had been deacquisitioned by a retired dentist. I was selling the teeth for five bucks apiece. Nick ended up taking fifteen or twenty of them. He put them in a little baggie and made his pitch.

"I'm really interested in this stuff, and I buy. I would love to get together with you and see what other pieces you might have that you're willing to sell."

We exchanged contact information, and when I had something I thought he might be interested in, I'd shoot him a text. We didn't socialize or spend time together, but that changed when I invited him over to my apartment to examine some pieces.

"Why don't you come over?" I texted. "I have a few random oddities for sale if you want to have a look."

Nick was interested, but he could only come over after 10 p.m., which was past my bedtime. I was in the habit of going to sleep early so I could hit the flea markets as soon as they opened, but I made an exception for Nick.

"See you at ten!"

When Nick arrived, I noticed a change in his personality. He seemed more amped-up than usual, which was saying something because Nick was a high-energy guy.

I showed him a few things, we quickly agreed on some prices, and he paid me in cash—about $5,000 total. When we were done, he flipped the script on me.

"Why don't you come over to my place and see *my* collection?" he asked.

This was new. I respected Nick because he hustled and was a shrewd negotiator. When I made the rounds at the flea markets, I knew I would bump into Nick at some point. He was always there.

A look inside Nick's apartment

For as long as I'd known Nick, he'd never invited me over to his apartment to see his collection. In fact, he didn't talk about his collection at all. Some collectors are show-offs, and some are secretive. A lot of young collectors today put everything online for all the world to see. Nick was the exact opposite. Whenever I saw him out in the field and asked him what he was looking for, he would get evasive and noncommittal, as if he were afraid I'd use the information against him in a deal someday.

I was definitely curious about his collection, and I suspected this was why he was in such a strange mood. Perhaps there was something in particular he wanted me to see, but it was already late and it was very cold outside, so I declined.

Nick, however, was persistent.

He made a point of telling me how much more evolved my collection was than his, insinuating that he was still a beginner at collecting oddities. I didn't believe that for a second. Sure, my collection was more extensive, but he was no novice. He kept telling me about a shrunken head that he wanted to show me, which I was, in fact, very interested in seeing.

"What do you say?" he asked.

With a great deal of reluctance and more than a little trepidation, I agreed to go with him.

"Let me grab my coat," I said.

I went into my bedroom and texted Regina.

"If you don't hear from me in an hour, you might want to come looking for me."

"What?"

The funny thing is that I'd only been dating Regina for about a month. I didn't want to freak her out, but Nick was acting a little strange, and I wanted to make sure that someone knew where I was going. To be fair, both Nick and I had acted out of character. This was the first time I'd invited him into my home, and now I was going to his, but I was starting to second-guess myself.

What have I gotten myself into? I thought.

As an extra precaution, I slid a switchblade into my pocket—an Italian pearl-handled stiletto—and headed out the door.

We went downstairs and headed to Nick's vehicle: a white van with no windows that was completely beat to hell. It looked exactly like the kind of murder mobile a serial killer would drive.

I took a deep breath. To succeed as a collector, you sometimes have to put yourself into uncomfortable or even dangerous situations.

You're sort of like an urban explorer in this regard. This was one of those situations where I felt it was worth the risk. The guy had just dropped five grand buying things from me. It was entirely possible that he had some incredible things in his collection that I might want. Plus, I really wanted to see that shrunken head.

So I got in the van, but the bad feeling wouldn't go away.

I kept one hand on the switchblade and the other on my phone. The van didn't have any heat and it was like an icebox in there. We were about ten minutes into the drive when I turned around and saw that we weren't alone.

There was someone sitting in the back of the van.

"What the—"

"Oh," Nick said, "that's my assistant."

The guy in the back didn't look right. He didn't look like an assistant; he looked like some drifter Nick had picked up off the street.

I felt like I was in a scene straight out of a 1970s serial killer movie. Why didn't Nick mention his assistant to me earlier? Why did Nick leave him in the frozen van the entire time he was in my apartment? Wasn't this how every mob movie ended?

I was so freaked out that when Nick offered me a cigarette, I accepted it—and I don't even smoke.

We finally got to his place in Carroll Gardens, Brooklyn. He lived in a four-story brownstone, third floor walk-up. As soon as we all went inside the building, I started to relax a little. I'd survived the trip. I figured that if he was going to kill me, he would have made his move by now.

He opened the door to his apartment, and I could see stuff spilling out into the hallway. Bags of clothes, dusty boxes, old furniture. We went inside, and it was more of the same. There was stuff *everywhere*.

My heart sank. Nick was a hoarder.

"Holy shit, Nick," I said. "How do you live like this?"

"It's a little cluttered," he admitted.

This wasn't clutter. This was a health hazard.

As I followed Nick down a pathway through the rooms, I could see that he had an exceptional eye. Among the piles of junk were some real standout pieces.

A glimpse into the weird and hectic world of Nick Parmesan. This photo was actually taken after some of the items had been moved out of the cluttered apartment. Shown is an early nineteenth-century artist's model sitting on an antique electric chair from a prison.

"How do you find anything in here?" I asked.

"I know where everything is," he said, which is what hoarders always say.

To prove his point, he produced the shrunken head—a well-preserved specimen from Peru—that I ended up buying from him.

That night is when our relationship began in earnest. I don't want to say "friendship"—that would come later—because he was so odd. We did a lot of business together over the next couple of years. He'd buy stuff from me, and I would occasionally buy from or trade something with him. I think he only sold things when he needed the cash to buy something else he had his eye on. He spent a lot of money with me, but those deals came with a lot of baggage.

Sometimes a few hours after I sold him a piece, he'd start texting me, usually late at night.

"I don't know about this piece, Ryan. I don't think this is a fair deal."

He was basically insinuating that I was trying to rip him off. I knew what he was doing. This wasn't buyer's remorse. He was trying to wear me down so I'd give him a better price the next time we did business together. Once the text messages started coming, they didn't stop, and I'd find myself spending the next several hours exchanging texts with Nick, trying to placate him until we ended up back where we started.

It would have been a shrewd move if he only did it once or twice, but he did it all the time. I was starting to understand why other collectors told me they'd never do business with Nick again. It got to the point where, after every deal, I'd get nervous, anxiously awaiting Nick's first text.

Then he started showing up at my house unannounced—we'd come home, and he'd be waiting on the stoop with a tray of chicken parm. He'd pretend it was a peace offering, but it was also a bargaining chip.

Nick's strange behavior continued. He started to get very aggressive. He didn't just complain about the price; he started claiming that items that weren't part of the deal had been left out. When I tried to convince him that he was mistaken, he would get verbally abusive with me. His texts got crazier and crazier. Then, when it seemed as if he'd completely lost it, he'd come back to his senses and apologize.

It became a pattern. I realized I was in an abusive relationship with this man. My dealings with Nick had turned totally toxic. The best chicken parmesan in the world wasn't worth this kind of behavior, and I had no choice but to cut him off.

"Look, you're a nice guy," I said, "but I can't do business with you anymore. We're done."

I blocked his number, and that was that. I didn't see him or talk to him for several years.

That was almost the end of the Nick Parmesan story, but then fate—or something—brought us together again.

<hr />

CARROLL GARDENS
Regina

After we were married, I moved into Ryan's apartment in Greenpoint for a few years. The whole time we were there, we talked about looking for a bigger place. Between his stuff, my clothes, two cats, one dog, and the ever-expanding collection, the apartment was just too small for us. I couldn't wait to get out of that place and move in somewhere more spacious.

We finally found a much larger apartment in Carroll Gardens. Technically, the apartment was four flours: three floors and a studio in the basement. We had a lot more room for the collection, and our bedroom was huge. Plus, I had a separate room for my boudoir.

Our new place was right around the corner from an old-school Italian deli that reminded me of Rhode Island. The whole family worked there, and everybody spoke fluent Italian. They had a picture of the pope on the wall, and the ninety-year-old patriarch of the family would sit at a table and watch a little black-and-white television.

Carroll Gardens, as you might know, was a notorious hot spot for the Italian Mafia. Joseph "Crazy Joe" Gallo, an infamous mobster and caporegime of the Colombo crime family, was once a resident. He reputedly kept an actual lion in his home to scare those who owed him money.

The deli opened at 6 a.m. and served breakfast—you could smell the bacon frying from our apartment—so we were in there all the time. Everybody in the neighborhood went there for breakfast. Students, construction workers, old-timers. It was that kind of place.

One day we went in there when they were pulling a tray of chicken parm out of the oven, and we knew right away that this was the place that Nick's family owned. We'd moved into Nick Parmesan's neighborhood. In fact, as we would soon discover, Nick lived three blocks away.

Great, I thought. *Now we're gonna have to deal with this guy again.*

We started to see Nick at the deli, which initially made me a little nervous because once Nick realized we'd moved into the neighborhood, he would stop by our apartment to say hello. One time he knocked on our window when I was home alone, which, to be perfectly honest, startled me and creeped me out.

In spite of all that, there was clearly something different about Nick. He seemed calmer, not nearly as manic, and much more subdued. He'd put on a little weight, but at the same time he somehow seemed more frail. Was he nicer to us because we were on his turf now?

We'd see him in various places around the neighborhood, and he was always very cordial to us. He would ask me about my mother, who was very sick at the time, and that really touched me.

We'd go into the deli and see Nick sitting at a table watching television, and we'd sit with him for a while. Sometimes I'd run back to our apartment to take a call, and Ryan and Nick would talk about antiques and oddities for hours.

After years of not speaking, we got to be on really good terms with Nick and reconnected on a much deeper level as friends. A lot of friendships are based on business. We have tons of acquaintances whom we do business with on a regular basis, but there's no real friendship there. It's more of a transactional relationship. With Nick, we needed a buffer between us where there wasn't any pressure to do business in order for our friendship to grow. Once we got to that point, our relationship came full circle.

A funny thing started to occur during our time in Carroll Gardens. Because we knew Nick and his family—who had lived there for many decades—we received special treatment. For instance, one time a cop tried to ticket Ryan for failing to move his car for street cleaning. The pizza guy across the street came out and shook his finger at the cop, who moved on without issuing the ticket. On another occasion, Ryan got into an argument with an aggressive neighbor on our block. Apparently, the neighbor received a "talking to," and after discovering that we were friends with Nick's family, he came to our front door and apologized to Ryan.

One day, Nick inquired if Ryan was interested in some items from his collection, which was something he'd always been reluctant to do in the past. Nick, like most hoarders, didn't like to get rid of *anything*. Slowly but surely Ryan and Nick renewed their business relationship, only this time around two things were different: Nick was much more mellow to deal with, and he was doing most of the selling. Nick was still acquiring objects for his collection, just not as often and rarely from Ryan.

One night at around nine o'clock, Ryan got a call from Nick.

"Can I ask you for a favor?"

"Sure, Nick," I heard Ryan say, "anything you need."

Nick had just bought a very heavy eighteenth-century cast-iron cemetery gate and needed help getting it up the stairs to his apartment. He came and picked Ryan up in his van. When Ryan returned, I could tell something had happened.

"Is everything okay?" I asked.

"Yeah," Ryan said, "that fucking thing weighed four hundred pounds."

I laughed as I tried to imagine Ryan and Nick struggling to get the cemetery gate up three flights of stairs.

"You wouldn't believe Nick's apartment."

Ryan explained that when they got to the top of the stairs, he could tell Nick didn't want him to come inside, but he didn't really have a choice because Nick couldn't get the gate inside his apartment by himself.

"He was embarrassed," Ryan told me.

Nick's apartment had been in bad shape before, but now it was a lot worse. There was hardly any room to walk, and all the usable space was dusty and dirty. That would have been a deal-breaker for me, but of course Ryan wanted to see what Nick had added to his collection.

More oddities from Nick's extensive collection

I liked the new Nick, but I worried about him. After hearing about the state of his apartment, it now made sense why he spent so much time at the deli: He literally couldn't go home. Ryan would help him do things from time to time, but mostly they hung out in the deli together, drinking espresso and shooting the shit like a couple of old guys from the neighborhood.

Nick was a hoarder, but he wasn't a shut-in. He didn't travel far, but he drove all over the Northeast in that white van of his. We would see him all over the place: flea markets, estate sales, auctions. He would just get in his van and go. He seemed to be everywhere.

Shortly before Nick passed away, we bought our house in Connecticut. We'd always wanted a place that could serve as a living museum for our collection, but I never imagined that place would be in Connecticut. Growing up in Rhode Island, I always thought of Connecticut as being in the way of New York, a state to pass through on the way to somewhere more exciting. When the opportunity presented itself to purchase an eighteenth-century Victorian home, we had to jump on it. As a result, we were no longer living in Carroll Gardens—so when Nick died, the distance allowed us to reflect on our relationship.

Nick's change in personality made a lot more sense to me once we learned that he had been sick. Nick knew he was dying and decided not to share that information with us or his family. That was his choice. I'm glad I got to know the kinder, gentler Nick because most people never got to know that person. I'm pretty sure a lot of people reading this who knew him will be surprised to learn about Nick's other side.

When we were leaving the neighborhood, Ryan had an exchange with Nick that struck him as strange at the time but made more sense after he died.

"If I ever get sick or decide to give up my collection," Nick said, "you'll be the first to know. I'm just not ready yet."

At the time, Ryan thought he was talking about his attachment to his collection, which is something that all collectors talk about. After Nick passed, Ryan realized Nick was probably thinking about his imminent demise. Even though Nick knew he was dying, he wasn't ready to part with his stuff.

This blows my mind. Imagine being at the end of your life and not being able to let go. I think about that all the time.

Naturally, Nick's death put his family in a terrible situation. His brother knew that he collected a lot of weird stuff because Ryan and

Nick usually did their deals in the deli. That's where they met to chat or discuss business because Nick didn't want anyone in his apartment. If Ryan was buying something, it would be at the deli, which his brother ran. They were always there.

Once we heard that collectors were moving in on the family, Ryan called Nick's sister, who was handling the estate, and they had a very emotional conversation.

Nick's family was under a great deal of pressure—and they were horrified by the state of their brother's apartment. I think they had a hard time coming to grips with how bad things had gotten. The family was very close—the deli brought them all together every day. Nick's sister lived just a couple of blocks away from her brother's apartment, but she had no idea that he was living in this cobweb-covered death trap.

Over the course of the conversation, it became clear that although Nick's sister knew the collection was valuable, she had no idea how to separate the trash from the treasures, which was completely under-standable. At that moment, we realized that Ryan was one of the few people who'd been in his apartment and the only one who'd bought and sold from him over a long period of time. For most people, deal-ing with Nick was a one-and-done type deal.

Ryan was in a position to be able to make a fair assessment of Nick's collection. He immediately started to write down every item that he remembered selling him or seeing in Nick's apartment because he'd been there three or four times during the course of their business dealings. It didn't matter how big or small the item was—Ryan put it on the list.

This is what we do every time we purchase a collection. We make an inventory and estimate its value. We do this to establish a ceiling to ensure we don't outbid ourselves. If you're buying an entire collec-tion, you need an inventory, even if it's just a partial one, so that the second someone makes an offer or asks you, "How much would you pay for it?" you have a basis for your answer. For every deal, you need to know two things: your initial offer, which is the starting point, and the number where you will walk away.

Ryan's notebooks are pretty much undecipherable to anyone but him. I can sometimes make things out, but they're overlaid with unique notations. For instance, let's say he's not sure if an item is part of a collection; he'll put an asterisk by it and then add another notation once he confirms it's there. Making lists is Ryan's obsessive way of getting everything out of his head and down on paper so he can start researching the objects that are up for sale. He'll look at news stories, academic articles, and auction catalogs. He'll go online, visit libraries, and call experts in the field—whatever it takes to learn what he can about the objects for sale. You have to go into these situations as prepared as possible.

The evening we spoke with Nick's sister, we had plans to celebrate Ryan's birthday. Instead, he drove down to Brooklyn to meet with her later that night, and she asked him to make an offer on Nick's collection, which Ryan was ready to do. There was a second component to his offer: We agreed to clear all the junk out of Nick's apartment and preserve any personal, family-related items that we found.

Nick's family accepted. I think they were relieved not to have to deal with his apartment. We were now the owners of the Nick Parmesan collection—and the mess that came with it.

———◆◆◆———

EXCAVATING THE COLLECTION
Ryan & Regina

We quickly realized that we'd bitten off more than we could chew. A lot more.

Nick's apartment was in terrible shape. Everywhere we looked, there were stacks of trash on the verge of toppling over and crashing to the floor. We had to wear masks when we were in the apartment— and it still smelled terrible. There was broken glass everywhere. We didn't understand how anyone could live like this.

Nothing about Nick's collection made sense. Nick had bags upon bags of white Wrangler shirts that still had the tags on them. Not ten or twenty, but a hundred shirts. He had boxes of beautiful, custom-made, leather-bound notebooks that had never been used. What was he planning to do with these things? Was he selling them?

We found a beautifully preserved Edison filament light bulb haphazardly wrapped in a plastic bag. Then we found another, and another. We found a total of three hundred antique light bulbs. Who needs that many old light bulbs? What was Nick going to do with them?

We could only speculate. It was impossible to know.

Nick's collection was filled with strange curiosities. The standout was a pair of incredible eighteenth-century Italian gilded putti sculptures that weren't like anything we'd ever seen before. They were angelic-looking infant boys, except they had weird faces carved into their stomachs that looked like demons trying to burst out of their bellies.

Were they a metaphor for out-of-control gluttony or desire? Perhaps, but this unique combination of the beautiful and the grotesque was incredible. The sculptures looked like metal statues but were actually made of wood. They were covered in a polychrome

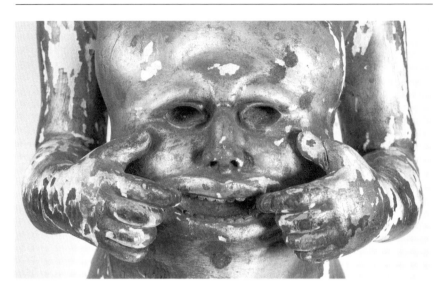

A detail of one of the eighteenth-century gilded putti statues

material that had been deteriorating for some time and was flaking off, adding a patina that made the pieces look that much more gruesome.

As a collector, Nick knew what he was doing. So how did things get so out of control in his personal life? Sorting through Nick's things provided us with a worst-case example of how quickly collectors can go overboard.

How do you know if you've bitten off more than you can chew?

How do you know when you've gone too far?

When is enough enough?

The clock was ticking, and we had to get to work. Complicating matters was the fact that we no longer lived in the city. Did we mention that this all went down in the middle of the pandemic?

It was a stressful situation. We hired a friend of ours—a sword swallower, an actual sideshow freak at Coney Island—and he assembled a crew of weird kids to help us clear out Nick's apartment. Remember, it was a third-floor walk-up in a very creaky nineteenth-century building. There were no elevators.

We had to separate the junk from the good stuff, which had to be handled with the utmost care, and then we had to haul the trash away. We drove the valuable items to our home, which was well over an hour away. It was a bittersweet moment when we carried the four-hundred-pound cemetery gate down the stairs—the same gate Ryan had helped Nick carry up the stairs all those years ago.

After three days of moving stuff down three flights of stairs and loading it into our cargo truck, we'd barely made a dent. There was just too much stuff, and we were running out of time. We were going to need professional movers.

Around this time, we got an urgent call from Nick's sister. The NYPD was searching for several firearms that Nick had registered. Had we found them?

We panicked, thinking that the police were going to turn Nick's apartment into a crime scene, but it wasn't that serious. Nick was a retired police sergeant and he had a permit for the guns, but his family was convinced they were hidden somewhere in the apartment. If someone were to find the guns and they ended up on the street, it would be bad news for everyone.

We'd seen plenty of deals get killed for less.

We informed everyone involved in the move—from our helpers to the cleaners to the movers—that we were looking for guns, but the only firearm we found in Nick's apartment was an antique Ruger. That clearly wasn't Nick's police weapon, but we gave it to his family anyway.

It took us three weeks to empty out Nick Parmesan's apartment and make it presentable again, but we got it done.

In a hoarder situation, there's a tendency to rush through things because of all the junk, but we had to be meticulous because we never knew what we'd find. We had to move quickly, but we also had to be careful to ensure that we didn't throw away something that looked like garbage but was actually incredibly valuable. To this day we are discovering objects that at first glance look like junk but are actually irreplaceable parts of another piece.

We'd paid a large sum of money for this collection, so there was an element of risk as well because we didn't know what kind of condition things would be in. It was a very stressful operation.

During this process of discovery, we found the paperwork that went with various objects: invoices, receipts, delivery orders, everything. Nick never threw *anything* away, and these papers helped us figure out what we were dealing with and, in many cases, provided us with the necessary provenance to help decipher what we had in our possession. We also made some sad discoveries about our old friend.

We found printouts of exchanges he'd had with various buyers and sellers at online auction sites, and in some cases the transactions had gotten very ugly. He would fight with people and was generally uncooperative when they had complaints about the items they bought from him. He had a reputation for being abusive in some online communities, and we found plenty of evidence that this was indeed the case—boxes and boxes of correspondence.

He was infamous in the community of Ouija board collectors, a group of people around the country who are obsessed with collecting vintage spirit boards, which first became popular in the late nineteenth century. When Nick's negotiations broke down with a mutual friend, Nick threatened to kill him and his children. It was really bad stuff. We found a package that was addressed to our friend with a vintage Ouija board inside it. We reached out to the poor guy and gave it to him. We didn't want any part of whatever bad blood there'd been between them.

That was the old Nick, the Nick who was bad with boundaries and let his anger overwhelm him. Our friend never got the chance to deal with the new Nick, and now he never would. We were saddened to learn that some people in the collecting community were actually celebrating the fact that Nick would never mistreat them again.

We don't think Nick was a bad guy. We think he put an intense amount of energy into collecting to the point where he would lose sight of everything else—the squalid condition he was living in was proof of that. His enemies think he was sick. His friends and family think he was misunderstood. We think he was afflicted, and whatever he had, we have it too. He had a mania for collecting that only

ODDITIES FROM THE NICK PARMESAN COLLECTION

- *Austrian chandelier made with real antlers*

- *Slipper owned by Abraham Lincoln made of Confederate currency*

- *Victorian papier-mâché skull made by famed artist Louis Thomas Jérôme Auzoux*

- *Futuristic art deco sculpture that would not be out of place in the film* Metropolis

- *Nineteenth-century parade suit of armor*

another collector can understand. That's why we got along so well: We understood each other.

That doesn't mean Nick wasn't socially awkward or difficult to deal with, because he was. One time we ran into him at Home Depot. We'd just bought a new car, and Nick was really impressed with it, so we gave him a ride back to his place. After we dropped him off, he started to send Ryan long texts. "You can't ever understand how jealous I am of your life, your space age car, your beautiful wife, your incredible collection . . ."

It was a little unsettling because we didn't know what he meant by it. Were these texts meant to be a sign of his admiration? If so, he had a strange way of showing it. As the texts kept coming in, it was clear that Nick had this fantastic vision of us that didn't reflect our reality. Our lives were far from perfect. We had our ups and downs, just like everyone else.

Ultimately, he looked up to us as collectors, but we believe he felt there was a rivalry between him and us because we were able to do something with our collection that he was not. We didn't really appreciate the extent to which we influenced his taste until we were able to move his entire collection out of his apartment. Once we had all his pieces together in Connecticut, we could truly see what he'd put together, how many of the objects were inspired by our own collection, how in sync our interests had become.

Another discovery: Nick got his start collecting vintage cast-iron cookware. That was his entry to the world of collecting. We found eBay printouts for eighteenth-century pans he'd purchased that cost anywhere from $5,000 to $25,000. Who knew that antique cookware was so valuable? Like anything else in the world of collecting, there happens to be a huge community of people obsessed with rare cast-iron cookware.

We were able to follow the paper trail and see when Nick started selling his cast-iron pans to fund purchases in the world of oddities, which was not unusual. When collectors lose interest in one field, it's usually because they've become obsessed with something else.

We were elated to find some documentation for the Witch's Door. Nick had bought the piece from a collector who had purchased the item at an auction in 2001 from the renowned antiquarian Roger Bacon. Bacon was an expert from Exeter, New Hampshire, who specialized in Pilgrim furniture and folk art antiques. He was, like many people, fascinated with witchcraft. The description of the piece was even more tantalizing.

The door was from Salem, Massachusetts, and dated back to the Salem witch trials of 1692. That meant the door was from a home where one of the women who had been accused of practicing witchcraft either lived or was imprisoned. Whether the woman was actually practicing witchcraft or a victim of mass delusion was beside the fact. The carving of the female witch image and the letters OLD JEF were meant to mark the house. These symbols essentially declared, "A witch lives

Detail from the Witch's Door. Inscribed are the words "Old Jef" and a crude carving of what appears to be a witch-like figure with cloven hooves.

here." In other words, the door bore a warning to passersby that there was a witch within.

The Salem witch trials represented an ugly chapter in American history. The phenomenon of accusing people of witchcraft was not limited to Salem or even Massachusetts. Quite a few witch trials took place in other colonies, such as Connecticut and New Hampshire. Nor was this widespread panic unique to New England. Witch trials transpired in Europe as well. In the context of the trials, *witch* did not refer just to women; men and even children were also accused of practicing witchcraft.

In Salem, two hundred people were accused of witchcraft, thirty were found guilty, and nineteen were executed. Of those killed, the majority were hung at Gallows Hill. The taint of being accused of witchcraft had long-term consequences for those who were spared the hangman's noose.

Naturally, we had a lot of questions. What did the markings mean? Did the symbols indicate the so-called witches were held against their will behind this door until they were brought to trial? Or was the door from the home of one of the two hundred people who'd been unjustly accused? If so, did the owner survive the ordeal? Was it possible to know the identity of the person to whom this door belonged?

Every time we look at the Witch's Door, we think of Nick. There were a lot of similarities between Nick's situation and that of the witches of Salem. He was regarded by the collecting community as something of a pariah; like those who were accused of witchcraft in Salem, he was treated like an outcast, someone to be shunned and even feared. When Nick saw the Witch's Door, did he feel that he too was misunderstood? Did he feel as though there was something sinister about his appetite for the esoteric and the macabre that caused him to live the way he did?

Cleaning out Nick's apartment and transferring his collection to our home in Connecticut prompted some soul-searching. We asked ourselves all kinds of uncomfortable questions that we're still considering today, but the question we come back to again and again is this: What's the difference between a collector and a hoarder?

To a certain degree, all collectors have a tendency to hoard. The difference between us and someone like Nick is that we display items from our collection. Our house is specifically set up like a living museum. The pieces we've collected are there to be viewed and enjoyed not only by ourselves but by anyone who visits our home.

But this is true for only part of our collection. Most people never see the things we have in storage—whether it's the items in our basement that aren't ready to be showcased, like Mr. Peepers, or the objects and artifacts from the large collections we purchase that we're still sifting through, trying to determine if we're going to sell them or keep them in our collection. We store these items temporarily in the chapel.

You're probably thinking it's weird that we would have a chapel, and it is, but it came with the property. Our house was once inhabited by a minister, and in the backyard sits an old chapel from the nineteenth century. How or why it was moved there is anyone's guess, but the first thing we did when we moved in was to paint it black. Today we use it as a staging area for moving objects in and out of the house.

A lot of Nick's stuff is still in the chapel, and when we're there, we think about him. Did he realize it when he crossed over from being a collector to a hoarder, or was it a gradual process? Did it feel like he'd been overtaken by his possessions?

Sometimes it feels that way to us. Sometimes one of us will say, "Let's sell everything and retire!"

It's a joke—most of the time.

Unfortunately, Nick's collection was so out of control that he couldn't do anything with it, which is a heavy, heavy thing. But it wasn't always that way.

One time he asked us for advice about ways he might display his collection. He asked about getting some shelves and cabinets built in his apartment. On some level, he knew it was impossible to go on living the way he did. He also had to know what a huge undertaking it would be to clear out his apartment in order to get shelves built, and that was probably scary to him. I don't know if he ever reached out to the carpenter we recommended, but it's safe to say that his plans for displaying his collection died when he got sick.

A few years have passed, and we're still going through his collection, still finding bizarre items. There were things in the collection that we initially thought would go for maybe a few hundred dollars, but then we would find something unique about them—a maker's mark or something special about the piece that made it ten times more valuable, but you would never know it by taking a quick glance at it. We had to teach ourselves to see things through Nick's eyes. We eventually came to trust our old friend's instincts: If Nick kept something, it was bound to have a rare or unique quality.

The interior of an animatronic head from Nick Parmesan's collection that was once used in the Stephen King miniseries *Rose Red*

For instance, we found an old shoebox of odd objects, including a lady's slipper made of paper. There was no rhyme or reason to the items in the box. Nothing looked particularly valuable, but it was all very old. It was only when we got to the bottom of the box that we discovered the thread that tied these things together: They all once belonged to Abraham Lincoln. The slipper was made out of shredded Confederate currency.

Presidential history isn't really our forte—who knows what these objects would go for at auction?—but it's absolutely fascinating that Nick had these incredibly rare objects stashed in a shoebox and buried under a mountain of garbage. What was he thinking?

After Nick passed away, it took a lot of time to go through everything in his collection. We laid out a significant amount of money to clean out Nick's apartment in a way that would give his family peace of mind. When you're dealing with a hoarder situation, you're tempted to get the job done as quickly as possible because of how unpleasant it is, but if you do that, you can miss out on some hidden gems. We didn't understand what drew Nick to collect what he did, but we held on to the idea that his issue was letting things go. In a weird way, we felt closer to Nick after he was gone than when he was here.

CHAPTER IX

THE
IRON MAIDEN

RETURN OF THE ODD
SIGNATURE STYLE
CANCELED
THE IRON MAIDEN

The Black Chapel

RETURN OF THE ODD
Regina

After *Oddities* was canceled, I needed to find a way to transition out of my corporate job in the fashion industry. Canceling *Oddities* was a mistake, but that's what everyone says when their show gets canceled. Sometimes getting canceled is a blessing in disguise because it frees you to do other things. I certainly felt that way because Ryan now had time in his life for a relationship with me, but it was clear that the public wasn't ready to let Ryan go. I had to come up with a plan both to evolve and to put him back in the spotlight.

We were involved in a flea market that was connected to a museum in Brooklyn, but the operation was running out of steam. The staff just didn't have the bandwidth to make it work. I would get so frustrated by how things were run because I saw so many opportunities to make it a success. I knew from my own managerial experience that more could be done to support the vendors, who are the lifeblood of any flea market, and to make the operation flourish.

I wanted to become more involved and asked if I could help manage the flea market. They basically handed me the reins.

"Just take it."

"Really?"

"You're gonna hate it."

I thought the flea market had the potential to be something special—if it was run the right way. I knew I had the tools to do it. I'd use my professional experience to treat the flea market like a real business. I was going to promote it and help the vendors make some real money. I figured that if I could sell $7 million a year in panties to people who didn't need them, I could do this.

The previous organizers weren't as optimistic. They didn't think it could be done.

"Have fun," they said.

I thought the flea market was the perfect vehicle for Ryan. It didn't make sense for Ryan to go out and find another television show just for the sake of being on the air, which a lot of well-known personalities do because they're afraid they will be forgotten. More often than not, they shift their focus in order to stay relevant and lose touch with the very reason why they were on television in the first place.

I knew Ryan didn't have to worry about that. He'd established a brand that was in sync with his passion for oddities. Viewers recognized that and responded to it. That's why he had the following he did, but he needed to pivot to something that would make the most of his platform and allow him to connect with those who shared his passion.

I thought Ryan should move on from unscripted television. He needed to do something creative so that he didn't become stagnant. The key was to avoid trying to replicate the success of the show and do something new. I felt the flea market could be the catalyst for the next chapter in Ryan's career, but it needed to be bigger—a lot bigger.

I could blow Ryan up on social media, which he was kind of clueless about. I could pair him with creators and collectors who looked up to him. I could make the flea market not just a place where you would buy and sell things but a place where you could hang out, listen to music, enjoy a cocktail, and meet cool, like-minded people. I imagined a space where people like us *wanted* to be. To do that, we had to expand the concept of what a flea market could be.

I wanted to change the way people perceived flea markets in the same way House of Wax had transformed the experience of going to the movies. I wanted to hold workshops, throw fashion shows, do live events, and make the market a highly curated space. I wanted people to know that Ryan was more than some guy on a television show who was an expert on old bones. He hadn't completely turned his back on making jewelry and exploding skulls, but he had so much more to offer as a collector and a curator.

I knew Ryan was ready for bigger and better things—and it was up to me to take him to the next level. All he needed was someone who could seize the opportunity, build the audience, and keep them coming.

In that spirit, the Oddities Flea Market was born.

The first Oddities Flea Market was held at Greenpoint's Brooklyn Bazaar in the spring of 2017 and was an overwhelming success. We partnered with our old friends Mike Zohn and Evan Michelson. We filled the Brooklyn Bazaar's three floors with unusual objects and unique antiques, and we had plenty of food and drink for our guests. Over three thousand people attended our debut, and they were lined up for eight blocks waiting to get in.

The turnout for the first Oddities Flea Market was so good that we had to keep it going. So many people showed up for the first event that not everyone who stood in line actually made it into the venue. We had to close the doors early to avoid overcrowding. We felt terrible about this, and to soften the blow we gave away the rest of our T-shirts to those still waiting in line.

We threw more events in Brooklyn to fine-tune the operation, and then we expanded to Los Angeles and Chicago. From there we set our sights on a few other cities, and that's when things really took off.

What makes the Oddities Flea Market different?

Glamour. I brought high fashion into what is typically a male-dominated space where women were all too happy to latch on to a fairly generic look that was part Goth, part Halloween. That, to me, felt like an artistic dead end. Oddities aficionados share many affinities with the Goth subculture, but I wanted to set a higher standard. I wanted people to dress up for our events but also be themselves and not feel like they were putting on a Halloween costume.

When I lived in West Palm Beach, my closest friends were the Goth kids from my high school, but I myself wasn't Goth. I've been the black sheep my whole life, but I also never felt like I needed to fit into a category. I didn't want to slap on white makeup or dye my hair black just to fit in with people who felt the way I did. If people were going to reject me, I wanted it to be because they didn't like me for who I was, not for who I was pretending to be.

After those early shows, young women reached out to me and thanked me for emphasizing fashion and elegance at our event. It was creepy *and* sophisticated, just as our wedding foretold. Now, when someone writes to me on social media, it's almost always to thank me for breaking the mold and not looking like a typical Goth person, which I think is really important because it established our goal for the Oddities Flea Market.

What I wasn't prepared for was to be thrust into the spotlight. When we started the Oddities Flea Market, my intention was to make it a showcase for Ryan. I thought I would be in the background, because that's where I've always felt the most comfortable, but there was this expectation that I would be part of the show because people loved our aesthetic together. We came to recognize that people liked Ryan and Regina *together* more than they liked Ryan and Regina *separately*. Plus, it was easier for Ryan if he wasn't the only face of the franchise.

Honestly, I don't think I was ready for the attention.

------◆◆------

SIGNATURE STYLE
Ryan

I suppose I should say a few words about my own sartorial style. When I first started collecting, I was a starving artist/rock and roll reject, and I looked like one.

Some of my early mentors, like Billy Leroy of Billy's Antiques, were sharp dressers, and I greatly admired them for it. It's something Billy tried to instill in me to a certain degree. Billy was a showman, and he looked the part. He looked like he belonged in the world he'd created.

Billy was originally from France, and he would travel to London for his tailoring. When he was a young man, any money he made went directly to the world-class tailors on Saville Row, the birthplace of bespoke suit culture. Once Billy developed his own style, he stuck with it. It didn't matter what he was doing. He could be out in the field, going to flea markets and antique shows—but he was always dressed to the nines.

What I took from Billy was not so much the way he dressed, but his commitment to dressing well. It wasn't something he did just for special occasions; he dressed well every day, which I appreciated and then embraced.

I didn't get into wearing expensive suits until my partners at Against Nature opened a bespoke suiting line. In the early days, when we didn't have customers, I would make jewelry for Jake and Amber, and they made suits for me. We'd wear each other's stuff to drum up business. They would make me any suit I wanted. That's when I started wearing three-piece suits regularly.

I've loosened up a little since we've moved out of the city. If I'm going out to the coffee shop, for example, I might wear a blazer or sport coat, but when I go out for dinner or an event, I always wear a suit.

It's my signature.

CANCELED
Regina

Early on, we decided to make every event we did unique. Whether we were throwing a party at House of Wax, curating an exhibition at a gallery or museum, or hosting the Oddities Flea Market, we wanted it to be special. It wasn't something we took lightly, and our events were so successful that we found ourselves in high demand.

We knew from the beginning that the Oddities Flea Market wasn't something we wanted to do every weekend or even once a month. We wanted it to feel like an event you marked on your calendar. If you missed it, you missed a one-of-a-kind gathering of creators, collectors, entertainers, and innovators that couldn't be duplicated and would never be repeated.

As our events gained steam, we noticed that people who came to the Oddities Flea Market saw each event as a chance not only to get dressed up but to express themselves in a unique way. This was especially true of guests who came to more than one of our events. They didn't dress like us—they dressed *for* us. In other words, they recognized that we were putting on a show for them, and they demonstrated their appreciation by putting on a show for us, which was incredibly cool.

I think that's one of the reasons why our events were so different. A lot of people came not for the oddities themselves but for the eccentric way people were dressed. Our guests went to great lengths to look amazing, which made for some exceptional people watching.

This is especially true of our events at the Globe Theatre in downtown LA, which are usually held

Ryan and Regina at one of the early Oddities Flea Markets at Brooklyn Bazaar in NYC

around Halloween. Our elegant and elevated aesthetic meshes well with spooky season. The costumes are extraordinarily well thought out. We've seen some pretty crazy outfits over the years, and it always makes me happy to see people go all out.

The early years of the Oddities Flea Market were an exciting time. We were experimenting, evolving, and expanding. We never wanted things to get stale. We constantly pushed ourselves to make things not necessarily bigger—though that happened as well—but better.

Little did we know that circumstances that would radically impact our ability to throw events were lurking around the corner.

In December 2019, we closed on our home in Connecticut and threw our last event of the year in Brooklyn. It felt like everyone got sick after the Oddities Flea Market. A bunch of friends told us over the holidays that they'd just gotten over the worst flu they'd ever had. And the "flu" seemed to spread easily. If event-goers shared a table with someone, they got sick. If they drove in a car together, they got sick. Looking back, it's pretty clear that the Oddities Flea Market was a super-spreader event, but we didn't have the words for that yet. No one did.

The coronavirus had arrived, but we didn't know anything about it yet. We would all become intimate in our own way with COVID-19, but no one had an inkling as to what lay in store as the calendar flipped to 2020.

In January, I had a sense that something big was coming. A lot of our vendors go to a huge international gem show in Arizona every January to buy the gemstones they'll need for the pieces they're planning to make that year. In Tucson, they learned that many of the dealers from Asian countries had skipped the show that year. Our vendors were told that there was "something going around," so most of the Asian jewelers stayed home. Even then, it sounded vaguely sinister. Something was clearly happening, and we knew it was only a matter of time before it came to the United States.

The Oddities Flea Market requires an enormous amount of planning. The events tend to sneak up on us because we're always looking so far ahead to secure the venue, curate the vendors, line up the entertainment, and so on. There's so much work that has to be done before we can even think about promotion or selling tickets.

We had booked venues in Brooklyn, Chicago, Los Angeles, and San Francisco for events in 2020. The Oddities Flea Market was officially a traveling affair. It wasn't like the circus, where entertainers travel with the same animals and perform the same tricks. We had different vendors and entertainers for every show, which took an incredible amount of planning. Securing the venues for these events required massive down payments of $10,000 or more, and when the venues canceled on us because of the coronavirus, many didn't refund the money. They kept it. That was on top of the lost income from ticket sales and vendor fees (we never take a commission on sales). There was also the hidden cost of the stock to sell at our events that was now sitting in our basement with nowhere to go.

Of course, the venues were struggling, but so were we. Of all the venues we worked with, only the one in San Francisco gave us our money back without a fight.

That was an eye-opener, an indication of how serious the situation was and how desperate things would become for so many people. But it was also a sign that we needed to do something—fast.

We were cutting checks every week to refund our vendors, but we weren't bringing in any money. It was frightening. We had no idea what we were going to do.

On the one hand, we felt incredibly lucky to have moved out of the city prior to the pandemic, but on the other hand, we were freaking out. We'd just bought a huge house, and with the lockdown in place, we couldn't hold our events. Now that our only source of regular income had been taken away, what the hell were we going to do?

There have been times in our lives when we had to make a decision quickly, and other times when we had to be patient. The pandemic required a little of both because we were in an unprecedented situation. We needed to pivot and try something new, but we needed to be strategic about it.

I had an idea. "We should do an online auction," I said.

Ryan was open to the idea, but skeptical. He was old-school and believed that online auction sites were the downfall of antique stores.

"We're not going to use those sites," I reassured him. "We're going to do it ourselves."

That got Ryan's attention, but he still wasn't quite convinced. It seemed like such an enormous undertaking.

"Let's just try it," I said.

We held a live online auction on Instagram, and it went so well we turned it into a weekly event. It was like a television show that we broadcast live from our living room every week, which we found hilarious in light of the comment I received after I got engaged to Ryan: "You know, Regina, life is not a show." From the Oddities Flea Market to our online auctions, our life has never stopped being a show.

People were stuck at home with nowhere to go and nothing to do. A lot of people were moving out of the city and buying new homes, and with so many stores closed, they desperately needed decor. Some people were simply tired of looking at the same four walls for months on end and wanted something to break the monotony. Then the stimulus checks hit people's bank accounts, and suddenly everyone had a little extra money to spend.

Every Saturday, we'd take a piece and display it live for the audience on Instagram. Ryan would talk about its provenance and point out the things he liked about it, basically generating interest in the piece. Our friend Paul Abrahamian did all the camera work, while I kept track of the bids, writing down the name of every bidder. Sometimes the winner of an auction would back out or their credit card company would decline the purchase, and I'd offer the item to the next highest bidder.

The auctions were a ton of work—each one lasted about three hours—but they were an absolute lifesaver for us. Ryan was sitting on all kinds of things he'd been buying for the purpose of selling at the Oddities Flea Market. While most of New York was shut down, we were still able to buy things locally in Connecticut. Because we held the auction every week, we were able to pick up on the types of things that were popular with our online audience, but you can never predict what will happen at an auction.

Sometimes a valuable piece would go for a lot lower than we thought it would. Sometimes a piece that wasn't particularly rare or unusual would command a high price. Sometimes it felt like people were buying things simply because it had been in our collection. And sometimes Ryan surprised even me.

One day, we were in the middle of an auction when Ryan announced, "It's time for the Bone Zone!" The Bone Zone was when we showcased whatever osteological specimens or preparations Ryan was selling that week. It was always at four o'clock and was usually the highlight of the auction because these items typically went for the highest prices of the day.

I was busy logging bids and taking down names. The work was fairly demanding, so I wasn't always paying attention to what Ryan was selling or what he had to say about it, but I paid close attention during the Bone Zone because the bidding was always intense.

Ryan pulled out a beautiful Tibetan piece, a gorgeous kapala.

I remember thinking, *Wow, that's really beautiful*, but also, *That looks kind of familiar.*

That's when it hit me: Ryan was selling the very same kapala that he'd offered me all those years ago when we first met!

"Are you seriously selling this right now?" I asked. I couldn't believe that Ryan was putting the kapala up for auction. It's literally what brought us together.

As Ryan nervously explained the story of the kapala to the audience, I was getting more and more pissed. I tried to hold it together, but I was obviously fuming. Naturally, the audience thought this was hilarious, and the bidding went through the roof. The more upset I became, the higher the bids went.

Ryan tried to play if off like an accident, like he didn't realize the significance of the kapala at the time, but he knew what he was doing. He always knows what he's doing. He's very meticulous that way. Even today, he justifies the sale with different explanations: He was raising funds to purchase another collection, or we got a lot more for it than the price he originally offered to me.

"That's beside the point," I said. "If it weren't for that kapala, we never would have met!"

"That's the name of the game, baby," he told me.

Whatever. It's not like we don't have plenty of other kapalas in the house. But this wasn't the first time he'd done something like this. He does this to me all the time. He sells things and replaces them with new objects without telling me, thinking I won't know the difference. Sometimes I don't, but I'm still pretty upset about that beautiful kapala.

We weren't the only people holding auctions during the pandemic. Antiquarians, art dealers, booksellers, and record collectors held online auctions during the lockdown and beyond. A lot of people in the antique business thrived during the pandemic, and many of them realized they didn't need their storefront operation anymore. They transitioned to selling on social media and never looked back.

"Why pay rent," they told us, "when I can do this from home?"

For many antiquarians, the pandemic changed the way they did business, so those were boom years for the industry. Our situation was different because our business was built around live events. We were fortunate to be in a position to provide some of the excitement of the Oddities Flea Market to our audience online.

It was a great experiment, but our auctions were a poor substitute for the Oddities Flea Market. We were able to pay our bills and strengthen our connection with our audience, and for that we will always be grateful. So many people told us, "Your auctions got me through the pandemic." A lot of the people who frequented our auctions now get together regularly and go to our live events together. It's a real community now.

As necessary as those auctions were to our survival during the pandemic, we are extremely happy to be doing live events again. The auctions helped us keep going, but the flea market is where the magic happens.

How long will we keep the Oddities Flea Market going? It's hard to say. I'm really proud of how much it's grown and what we had to overcome to keep doing it. We started small and kept working things out, and we'll keep growing until the universe tells us it's time to do something else.

Paul Abrahamian with Ryan from one of the many live auctions during the pandemic

One thing I know is that Ryan and I will never give up. Like all couples, we have our differences from time to time, but we are united by our black sheep bond. Neither one of us had the opportunity to go to college. We were both the oddball of the family, the one who was slightly out of step with the rest of society. We worked our way up from nothing. We are driven by our willingness to work, our belief in each other, and our desire to be successful because we are completely on our own. That's the bond we still share.

THE IRON MAIDEN
Ryan

The Oddities Flea Market was shut down for nearly two years. After the pandemic's restrictions on live events were lifted, we were so happy we threw an epic party in Los Angeles. We hired actors to dress up in terrifying costumes. We had performers on stilts, drag queens, monsters. That event was our biggest by far, and afterward we were exhausted.

After we wrapped up the Oddities Flea Market, we rented a big house in Malibu for a few days to unwind, and that's when I had an opportunity to purchase an antique iron maiden replica. But first a little background.

In Tim Burton's 1999 film *Sleepy Hollow*, it's revealed that Ichabod Crane, known for his encounter with the headless horseman, carries a dark secret. He witnessed his father, the Reverend Crane, murder his mother, Elizabeth, by placing her in an iron maiden—a casket-shaped torture device with iron spikes that point inward and impale whoever is imprisoned within it. Why did Reverend Crane murder his wife in such a barbaric fashion? For the sin of practicing witchcraft.

This grisly little detail does not appear anywhere in Washington Irving's short story "The Legend of Sleepy Hollow," which was published in 1820. In fact, iron maidens were not used in New England or anywhere else in the United States. Burton was likely inspired by Roger Corman's 1961 film *The Pit and the Pendulum*, which was based on a short story of the same name by Edgar Allan Poe. In the film, an iron maiden is used to great dramatic effect even though, once again, there's no mention of one in the original story.

The Pit and the Pendulum is set in the sixteenth century at the height of the Spanish Inquisition, a bloody chapter of European history during which heretical confessions were extracted by means of gruesome torture. Surely the inquisitors used the iron maiden to extract confessions from their captors, right?

Probably not. Medieval scholars maintain that there's no evidence that iron maidens were used during the inquisition in Spain—or anywhere in Europe for that matter.

Most people agree that the myth of the iron maiden began in the nineteenth century with a story that was told as fact. As the story spread, replicas of these devices were created. As the idea of medieval torture chambers took hold in the popular imagination—thanks to wax museums, movies, and even cartoons—iron maidens became a fixture in these houses of horror. No torture chamber was complete without one.

Despite its supposedly bogus history, I'd been on the hunt for an iron maiden for a long time. The more elaborate replicas were created so that the outside of the sarcophagus resembled a maiden. The best example of this is an iron maiden that was part of the extensive torture collection at Nuremberg Castle.

Regina and I were supposed to be relaxing in Malibu with friends when she received a link on Facebook marketplace from a colleague. There was a guy down in Orange County who had an iron maiden for sale, and he wanted a fortune for it.

I called him up right away and negotiated with him over the phone until we landed on a price that we were both comfortable with. He provided some details about the maiden's history and where it had come from, but it wasn't a lot. He had the piece in a storage facility in Orange County. We set up a time to meet that evening and drove down from Malibu.

The deal almost didn't happen because the guy was two hours late. We were getting ready to drive back to Malibu when he finally showed up, and he was really scary looking. We were both a little frightened of him.

The maiden was indeed a replica, like all iron maidens, but antique examples are quite rare, and this one was in great condition. You wouldn't think there would be so much demand for replicas, but because the perception persists that they were commonly used in torture chambers all over the world, interest remains very high. Ripley's Believe It or Not! has a nice one at their location in Manhattan. I was eager to add this piece to our collection.

This was actually not our first iron maiden. We have several miniature replicas that were sold as trinkets in the late nineteenth century in Nuremberg. Even though they're very small, they're still hard to find and sought-after by collectors.

After we completed the sale, we had to figure out a way to get it across the country on a flatbed truck, which was funny. Even though it was covered in tarps, the shape had a distinct coffin-like appearance. Anyone who grew up watching vampire movies would have been suspicious of the truck's cargo.

On delivery day, the iron maiden didn't arrive in Connecticut until nearly midnight. Watching it being carried across my yard in the moonlight and disappear inside the chapel was really fun, exactly like a scene from an old Vincent Price movie.

The maiden looks enormous from the outside, but it was designed with smaller people in mind. In the movies, the spikes impale the victim as soon as the door is closed, and then the poor person trapped inside bleeds out and dies. This specimen isn't as scary looking, but is a little more macabre. If I stand perfectly straight, I can fit inside it just fine, but as soon as I get tired and start to slump, it would be over. I'd be a human pincushion. So there was a level of psychological torture as well as physical.

A reporter from *Antique and Arts Weekly* once asked if she could get inside.

"How's your posture?" I asked.

The spikes aren't that sharp, but it's definitely a tight fit. I don't know what it is about the iron maiden, but people have a morbid curiosity about what it would be like to be trapped inside.

THE
RICHARD
HARRIS
COLLECTION

Seventeenth-century architectural marble relief from a French church. From the collection of Richard Harris.

MEMENTO MORI
Ryan

One of the most interesting things about being a collector of oddities is that if you stick with it long enough, you'll develop relationships with fascinating people from all over the world. Wherever we go, we can count on spending time with others who are similarly drawn to the odd and the unusual. It's like a vast and far-ranging tribe. When we curate an event in a distant city or take the Oddities Flea Market on the road, it's gratifying to connect with people who share our passion. Whether it's a new fan who is just getting started with her collection or a dealer we've worked with for decades, we come back from these encounters energized and inspired.

When we returned from the Oddities Flea Market at Morgan Manufacturing in Chicago in the spring of 2023, I asked Regina if she'd seen art dealer Richard Harris or his wife, Barbara, at the event. I was positive we'd invited them to the show and that we'd put them on the guest list, but neither Regina nor I could remember seeing either one of them. Come to think it, Richard hadn't responded to our invitation. That wasn't like him because he usually replied to me in a day or two. Even if I just sent him an email asking, "Hey, how have you been?" he always responded fairly quickly. We had that kind of relationship.

Something started to gnaw at me. I went through my emails to check the last time we'd corresponded, and I realized that I hadn't heard from him since before the pandemic. I fired off an email, but now I was concerned. I needed to know if Richard was okay. I did a quick search online, and that's when I discovered that he had passed away just three weeks prior. Right around the time when I'd sent off an invitation, he was transitioning into that other realm.

This was terrible news. Richard was both a first-rate collector and a friend. He had the finest collection of memento mori artifacts in the world. *Memento mori* is Latin for "Remember you must die." In the field of antiquities, a depiction of death—whether it's a sculpture, a death mask, or a work of art—that encourages the viewer to reflect on the transience of life and our inescapable fate is considered a memento mori.

The phrase dates back to ancient Rome, where it served as an upbeat reminder to make the most of the moment because it wasn't going to last. "Remember you must die" was the rough equivalent of "Enjoy life while you can." This sentiment was co-opted by the Christians in the Middle Ages, when life was short and death was everywhere, as a reminder that eternal damnation awaited those who reveled in sin. It encouraged believers to live a just and pious life to ensure the rewards of eternal salvation. Life is fleeting, but eternity is forever.

Each culture and every age has its own form of memento mori. From Victorian postmortem photography to Día de los Muertos (Day of the Dead) in Mexico, all of humanity is engaged in a never-ending conversation with death. No matter if you're rich or poor, famous or forgotten, revered or scorned, death is the final act for us all. We deal with the deaths of those dearest to us so that we may keep them alive in our memories and then somehow find the courage to keep going with the knowledge that death will one day come for us too.

Modern society has a much more clinical approach to death. The dead are ferried—not to the underworld—but from a sterile hospital bed to the mortuary to the church to their final resting place in the ground by a string of professionals who "spare" loved ones from having to come face-to-face with the grim realities of what happens to us when we die. Where once death was local—people were buried in the communities in which they lived by their families and neighbors—now the business of death has been farmed out to professionals who treat death like any other service industry. By outsourcing death, we have become disconnected from it, even though the most natural outcome for any living thing is to die.

As a result, modern-day collections of memento mori are often saddled with adjectives like *creepy, morbid*, and *macabre*. For example, death masks were once a popular way of preserving someone's likeness before their body started to decompose. These masks weren't considered the least bit odd. In an age when there were few ways to capture what someone looked like, death masks were a form of remembrance and were no more morbid than displaying a portrait of a deceased loved one in the family home. Today, most people consider death masks to be morbid, even though when we turn on our televisions at night we bear witness to death after death after death.

Despite what many people would like you to believe, memento mori isn't a subcategory for creepy collectors. Rather, collections of memento mori illuminate our relationship with death and help us come to terms with our final destination. No collector did more for memento mori than Richard, and now he was gone. How, I wondered, would *he* be remembered?

I met Richard through the show *Oddities*. We were filming in Chicago and did a short feature on the art dealer. He was in his mid-seventies at the time and in excellent health. Richard was a legendary figure in the world of oddities because he'd spent millions and millions of dollars building his vast collection, and it was worth considerably more than what he'd invested in it. It was regarded as one of the finest, most cohesive collections of memento mori in the world.

We filmed the show at his home, and afterward he and I were able to chat while Barbara prepared some food. It was a very pleasant afternoon. I was a huge admirer of Richard's collection before we met, but I became an even bigger fan of the man himself afterward.

As I was talking to him, I kept looking around, hoping to see some of the pieces from his collection, but I didn't see any of his masterpieces on display. I had to ask him about it. "I've heard so much about your collection," I said, "but you don't seem to have any of it in your home."

"No," he said with a laugh. "My wife and I have a deal. I can buy as much of this shit as I want, but I can't bring it into the house!"

I tried to wrap my head around spending all that money on beautiful works of art and not being able to enjoy them. He told me that most of his collection was sitting in an art-handling storage facility. I imagined a warehouse in Chicago like the last scene in *Raiders of the Lost Ark*, with row upon row of priceless artifacts and treasures hidden away in dusty crates. I was sure it was nothing like that, but I felt something like sadness for these objects that had been lost to time and then found by Richard, only to be hidden away again in a storage facility.

Throughout the years, I've thought about Richard's arrangement with Barbara on numerous occasions. In some ways, I'm never not thinking about it. When I met Regina, she basically walked into what must have looked to her like a hoarder's museum. Every collector has a different relationship to their collection. When two people share a space, they're going to have different views on how that space should be shared, from the stuff that goes into it, to how it should be displayed, to what should be done with it after they're gone.

Sometimes I lie in bed at night and think, "What if we sold everything and moved to Italy?"

I imagine a minimalist setup devoid of clutter. It's not a complete fantasy. We also have a cottage on our property that we use as a guesthouse, and the furnishings are sparse and the walls are bare. It's a stark contrast to the maximalist hell that is our home. The cottage is where we go when we need to get away from all of our stuff, a place to pretend we are normal people with normal lives who live in a normal home. What if we had a whole house that was like that, a second home that was as clean and modern as Richard's? Would I be happy in a place like that, or would I get obsessed with something new and start the process over, slowly filling it up with stuff?

After I found out about Richard's passing, I looked through all the books and exhibition catalogs I owned that displayed his pieces. He had generously allowed his collection to be photographed and published in various books about memento mori, though it was far too vast for a single volume to contain it all.

The best of these books is called *Death: A Graveside Companion*, which was produced by the publishing arm of the Morbid Anatomy Museum and edited by Joanna Ebenstein. The book is a collection of essays and is illustrated with examples of memento mori. I originally bought the book thinking the images showcased examples of memento mori from various museums around the world, but that wasn't the case. Nearly all of the images were from Richard's own collection, with other examples of memento mori, including one of my own pieces. Even though the essays span several centuries and many cultures, the depth and breadth of Richard's collection was so vast that he had examples of virtually all the ways death had been represented dating back to the beginning of recorded history.

What did he have?

In a word: everything.

Just about every rare piece of memento mori I've ever seen in a European museum, Richard owned. He had a seventeenth-century painting by Adriaen van Utrecht that's considered an early representation of vanitas, which is a work of still life that concerns the transitory nature of existence. He had a stunning collection of rare prints from masters like Albrecht Dürer, Francisco Goya, and Rembrandt. He also owned an entire series by the Weimar artist Otto Dix, who captured the madness of the First World War.

Richard was fascinated with anatomy and had books by anatomist Frederik Ruysch, illustrations from sixteenth-century Dutch masters, and photographs of nineteenth-century anatomists posing with cadavers. Richard had osteological and ethnographic artifacts that ranged from ancient Incan skulls to eighteenth-century Tibetan masks. He possessed an astonishing range of photographs of people dressed as skeletons: from the Ladakhi "death dancers" of the Himalayas to early twentieth-century trick-or-treaters in Chicago to Graciela Iturbide's images of Day of the Dead processions in Oaxaca, Mexico.

He also had beautiful sculptures, from modern representations of death made by contemporary artists, like Roger Reutimann's 6½ foot bronze sculpture *Death of Venus*, to seventeenth-century fruitwood carvings of skeletons wielding a scythe—a symbol for the inescapability of time's march. I'd seen a similar wood carving at a museum in Amsterdam, and it stopped me in my tracks. It was only about 11 inches tall, but it was stunningly intricate. I tried to find another like it and came across a listing for a similar sculpture that had been owned by Yves Saint Laurent and Pierre Bergé that sold at Christie's auction house for $150,000.

Richard had two of these beauties.

Richard even had several chandeliers made out of hundreds of plaster-cast bones, and each chandelier weighed over a ton. I wouldn't know what to do with something like that. In my mind, it belonged in the great hall of a warrior king, not in a box in a temperature-controlled warehouse in Chicago. I can only imagine Regina's reaction if I brought something like that home.

Close-up of the original pen and ink drawing entitled *The Triumph of Death* dated 1565 by Marinus van Heemskerck. From the collection of Richard Harris.

As I thought about all the priceless pieces in Richard's collection, I couldn't help but wonder what was going to happen to them all. To his dying day, his dream was to put his entire collection in a single place that would do it justice, but that was easier said than done. He tried to find a museum, university, or cultural institution that would take on his collection, but it was simply too vast for a single organization to handle. It sounds astonishing when you consider that he was willing to donate a collection he'd spent millions on, but showcasing all the pieces was an undertaking that would require several million more to do right.

Because Richard didn't have a way to display his collection, he was eager to share it with the public through exhibitions, which he did a handful of times during his lifetime. Richard showed parts of his collection at the Figge Art Museum in Davenport, Iowa, in 2010–2011;

the Chicago Cultural Center in 2012; the Wellcome Collection in London in 2012–2013; the C. G. Boerner Gallery in New York in 2016; and the Kenosha Public Museum in Kenosha, Wisconsin, in 2018. These traveling exhibitions represented a small sample of the vast treasures that Richard had amassed over the years. For example, the exhibition at the Wellcome Collection, "Death: A Self-Portrait," which was seen by over 136,000 people, consisted of three hundred pieces, which was just a fraction of his collection.

Of all the exhibitions, the one he did in his hometown of Chicago was the most grandiose. The exhibition, called "Morbid Curiosity," was twice the size of his presentation at the Wellcome Center. "Morbid Curiosity" was a landmark event in the world of oddities and was Richard's crowning achievement. Besides the collection itself, this exhibition is probably what he's best known for in the collector community. If you were serious about collecting memento mori, you went to see "Morbid Curiosity."

Richard told me about his struggle to donate his collection to various museums and that no one would take the whole collection off his hands. It was simply too big, too vast, too valuable. Nor was it something he could handle himself. The collection was too massive for him to be able to display on his own without the assistance of an extensive support staff.

It's the dilemma that all collectors face at the end of their lives: What are they going to do with their collection?

Every collector—whether it's Richard Harris or an elderly woman obsessed with commemorative spoons—wants to keep the collection intact. For serious collectors, every piece that you acquire is like a brushstroke on a canvas, and every time you add to it, you're creating a masterwork that's greater than the sum of the parts. A lot of collectors think of their collection as their masterpiece, and Richard's collection really was. It wasn't just the best collection in the world—it was the greatest of all time. His collection deserved its own museum with Richard's name displayed on the front: the Richard Harris Museum of Memento Mori.

Richard's situation was not without irony. He'd spent a great deal of time and money amassing a collection concerning death, and he wanted to find a home for it so that others could appreciate it after he died. This is the end goal of every prolific collector. You want your masterpiece to be celebrated and viewed for generations to come. You want your collection to live longer than you do. It's a way to cheat death. It's ironic, given the countless paintings depicting Death warning wealthy old men that they can't take it with them. Indeed, Richard owned several of them.

The last thing he wanted was for his masterpiece to be broken apart so the pieces could be sold to the highest bidder. That's what Richard was trying to prevent, but after he got sick, he had no other choice. When he passed away at the age of eighty-five, his collection was bequeathed to his family with instructions to sell the individual pieces at auction. In some ways, Richard's situation wasn't all that different from when Nick Parmesan passed away. His life's work was now someone else's burden.

Although Richard's circumstances were very different from Nick's, the outcome was similar. All collectors are obsessive and will stop at nothing to get what they want. In this regard, collectors, big and small, are secretive by nature. Case in point, Richard had continued to acquire pieces right up until he became ill. After he died, his daughter found hundreds of additional pieces that hadn't been cataloged. They were stored in the basement, in closets, and even under the bed. Barbara hadn't known anything about them. Richard had bought them on the sly.

This is what happens when one's compulsion to collect overshadows the realities of one's own existence. Even though Richard had reached the limit of what one person could handle—much less enjoy—he kept going.

I've felt that compulsion.

Nick succumbed to it.

Even Richard, with all his resources, was powerless to prevent it.

I know that Richard cared a great deal about his legacy. The last time we chatted, we talked about doing an exhibition together in New York. We were going to take part of his collection and part of my collection and bring them together for one big exhibition of memento mori. He'd already reached out to a few places in New York, but the venues were just too small to accommodate the scope of what we wanted to do. I started to look around, but we couldn't find a place in New York where such an exhibition made sense. Then came the pandemic, and everything shut down. Our joint exhibition never happened.

I sent an email to Richard's daughter, Leslie, to express my condolences and inquire about the collection. I suspected Richard's family would have many of the same issues selling the collection that he had encountered in his struggles to exhibit it: No single entity would be ready, willing, or able to handle a collection of that size. I had no expectation that Leslie would get back to me. I was just an acquaintance of her father's, one of many collectors who had a tremendous admiration for him and his collection.

Leslie did reply, though, thanking me for reaching out to her. She informed me that Richard had decided to break up his collection and sell it at auction. Once he got sick—Leslie told me he had cancer—he realized he was going to have to give up on his dream of donating the entire collection to an institution that would appreciate it. That must have been a very hard thing for Richard to come to terms with.

She also told me that the process of selling off his collection was already underway and had begun before Richard passed away. In fact, his library of rare books was up at Bonhams, a large, privately owned auction house that was founded in 1793 and now had offices in London, New York, Los Angeles, and Hong Kong. I looked up the auction site online and nearly fell out of my chair. Richard had a huge collection of books pertaining to anatomy, memento mori, and Dances of Death. Richard's collection rivaled the rare book holdings of any library or museum. We're talking the absolute cream of the crop.

I saw that a single book from Richard's library had already sold for the sum of $75,000. Keep in mind that this was just one out of several thousand pieces in Richard's collection. I did more digging and found some old auctions where Richard spent six figures on a single purchase.

This was discouraging news. Auctions are the kiss of death for private collectors because it means the best pieces will command a small fortune. This is, of course, good for the owner but challenging for small, independent collectors. There was no way we could compete with that.

Original oil painting entitled *Death and the Miser* by the Flemish painter Frans Francken the Younger from 1635 from the collection of Richard Harris. This painting depicts Death serenading a wealthy man with his foot resting on an hourglass.

I didn't lose all hope of acquiring pieces from Richard's collection, though. Auction houses, especially the good ones, are very selective. They will only take on what they believe will attract interest from the most bidders. After going through Richard's collection, they would determine which pieces would perform well at auction, and they would leave the rest to his family. I continued to speak with Leslie and learned that the Harris family would not be putting everything from the collection up for auction. Osteological and ethnographic pieces, which Bonhams was unlikely to take because it considered them too lowbrow, were going to be withheld.

I mentioned to Leslie my discussions with her father about holding a joint exhibition of our collections, which she was very enthusiastic about. She was also interested in preserving her father's legacy and investigating the possibility of sending a representative cross section of pieces to an individual or institution that had the ability to showcase her father's collection of memento mori. I suggested that was something Regina and I were in a position to do, and we discussed the possibility of memorializing her father through a joint installation, exhibition, or online display.

She sent me a catalog of her father's collection and asked me to go through it and indicate which pieces might be of interest. She told me I had to be quick about it. Bonhams needed time to pick up the pieces, sort through them, catalog each artifact, and prepare them for auction. There was a great deal of work that needed to be done in a short period of time, and the process was already underway.

I opened the document as soon as she sent it. Richard's private catalog had detailed descriptions of each piece in his collection, including when and where it had been purchased as well as how much he'd paid for it. This was the document the auction house would use to put together their catalog. As far as I knew, I was the first and only private collector to get this inside look at Richard's collection.

The catalog contained thousands of images—over twenty thousand. I spent the next few days in a fugue going through the catalog and making my wish list. Just one of Richard's pieces would be a major addition to my collection, and to consider several acquisitions was dizzying. But my feelings went much deeper than that.

After learning more about Richard and going through his collection more thoroughly, it dawned on me that not only was his collection of memento mori the best in the world—I believe he was the most prolific collector of this subject matter that ever existed. I've known a lot of collectors, but I'd never seen anything like this. Richard's collection was indeed worthy of its own full-scale museum, and it would be an extremely popular attraction. I wished I were in a position to make that happen for him.

I also realized that Richard, Nick, and I were all the same: We each had the same affliction. There were differences, of course. I didn't have Richard's means to acquire pieces, and Nick lacked my ability to display them, but we all had the same type of mind; we were all united by our obsessions. As I went through Richard's collection, my entire view of what we do changed in an instant. It wasn't about an individual compulsion to acquire, I realized, but a vision that we shared.

BRINGING IT HOME
Regina

Ryan made plans to go to Chicago to meet with Richard's wife and children and talk about his collection. The plan was to meet for dinner and share stories about Richard and his passion for collecting. In typical fashion, the timing couldn't have been worse.

Prior to leaving, Ryan had to prepare for the antique show in Brimfield, Massachusetts, which is the largest show of its kind on the East Coast. He'd also committed to creating four new pieces of art for a gallery show in Seattle, Washington, later that year, which would require a tremendous amount of focus. With all the time he'd been spending with Richard's catalog, he had to work like a madman to finish the pieces on time. Ryan will tell you that he works best with a deadline, and I've found this to be the case, but this time he really had to push himself. It was incredible to watch his process and see the artwork come together. Ryan makes only a few pieces of art a year, but they are always astonishing. I wish he had time to make art more often.

Shortly after he got back from Brimfield, we left for a short but long-overdue trip to Sicily, which we really needed because we'd been cooped up all winter. Toward the end of the season, our boiler had broken down, and we went without heat for an entire month. We had to hole up in our cottage with all of our dogs just to stay warm.

Between the broken boiler and everything that was going on with Richard's collection, Ryan considered postponing the trip.

"Don't even think about it," I said to him.

There's no way I was going to let him cancel our flights. I insisted we go. We're happiest when we're traveling and exploring new places together, but I feel like every time we schedule a vacation, some big deal goes down that threatens to derail it. As soon as we book a trip, the offers come out of the woodwork. It happens every single time.

We found ourselves in a strange little village in Sicily called Castelmola. It's possibly the tiniest town in all of Italy—certainly the smallest village we've ever visited. There's a modest church, a couple of restaurants and bars for the tourists, and that's it. People move up there because it's the highest point in Sicily and has some of the best views on the island, but I think the real reason people move to Castelmola is to be left alone. There's a place called the Bar Turrisi where literally everything is in the shape of a penis, including the liquor bottles.

Castelmola was so far away and so isolated that it was the perfect place to reflect on the astonishing developments of the last few weeks. Ever since we learned of Richard's death, Ryan had been in constant communication with the Harris family. After hours of discussion, he was able to procure a portion of Richard's collection for the purpose of creating a joint exhibition—just as Ryan and Richard had discussed before Richard became ill. Not just one or two pieces, but over a hundred.

This would be different from any other collection we've ever acquired. We were adding these pieces for the purpose of memorializing Richard's legacy. Now we would be using our collections to celebrate Richard and ensure that the memory of his achievements lived on, which is every serious collector's dream.

It was both an incredible honor and an awesome responsibility. To be entrusted with the legacy of a collector like Richard was a testament to all the hard work we'd put into showcasing not only our own collection but also the work of other artists through the Oddities Flea Market. I've always said that the flea market is about the artists, and now our reputation as curators was being recognized and rewarded.

Would this collaboration be housed in an existing museum or gallery, or would it be a traveling exhibition like Castan's Panopticum? Would there be a catalog, or could we expand it into a luxurious coffee-table book? What if we opened our own public museum? Was such a thing even possible?

We had no idea.

Before Richard passed, he'd discussed his plans with Ryan in great detail. They already had the concept mapped out. Richard had kept everything from his previous exhibitions, so we had all the copy and imagery we needed to promote the material. We just had to find an organization or institution that was as passionate about this stuff as we were. Even though Richard was gone, the mission remained the same: to get his collection out of its crates and into a place where the public could see it.

People always say to us, "We want to see your collection. We want to see things that we've never seen before, and we want to see it in person!"

A joint exhibition would be an excellent opportunity to get both
of our collections in front of our fans. No one else has what we
have, and while this is true of any collection that contains artwork or
antiques, we have an abundance of it. I think that's what separates us
from other collectors. Now we had an opportunity to do something
new on a scale that was bigger and grander than anything we'd ever
tried to do before.

As we walked the streets of Castelmola, there was no doubt in
our minds that we could do it. Whether it's a gallery installation, an
exhibition at a museum, or the Oddities Flea Market, curation is
behind everything we do.

Even though we had no idea where this exhibit would be held
or what it would look like once we put our collections together, we
knew what needed to be done, and we knew we would be able to pull
it off. We knew we could mix the two collections together to create
a beautiful, cohesive exhibition. We knew there would be headaches
with permits and insurance and shipping and ticketing and a hundred
other hassles, but we were ready for the challenges ahead. We'd been
building up to them our entire lives.

In the meantime, there was just one question lingering in the
back of my mind: How the hell were we going to fit all this stuff
into our house?

On the top floor of our house was a more or less unfinished room that
we seldom used. The last full-time occupant was our foster cat, Wolfie.
It had high peaked ceilings, and our plans for the space changed over
time, from turning it into a Moroccan-themed room to the place
where we put all of our natural history items. We decided to put the
things from Richard's collection in there—a Richard Harris wing,
if you will—but it needed a ton of work. When it was still Wolfie's
room, my friends and I painted his name on the wall and drew lots of

pictures of cats and cat heads. It was basically my rendition of New York City graffiti culture, but the theme was felines. That shows you how naive I was when we first moved into the house. I thought the house was so big that we could devote an entire room to a cat.

As soon as we got back from Sicily, I started making arrangements to renovate the room to get it ready for the collection. Ryan didn't share a ton of details with me about Richard's collection, but he did show me images of a few of the pieces that we'd acquired, and they were massive. Although there was room for Richard's stuff, there was no way we were going get everything up three flights of stairs to the attic, so we had to reconfigure a few things.

We decided to turn our primary bedroom on the second floor into a library. This was an easy decision to make since we each have our own bedroom. (One of us snores, and his initials are RMC.) It seemed kind of indulgent for one of the biggest rooms on the second floor to be empty most of the time. So we moved all of our books and bookshelves out of the library and into the primary bedroom.

The old library is now the official Richard Harris Room. Although the new library is bigger, it has less wall space because of all the windows. The library doubles as our office. Ryan finally has the space to spread out all his books and research materials when we're closing a deal. The Charlie McCarthy dolls that sit on the fireplace mantel keep Ryan company while he's working.

As for the top floor, I planned to turn that into my bedroom. I wanted a sanctuary at the top of the house. I wanted it to be as far away from all of our stuff as possible. I wanted a room where the walls were painted black, and I could sleep to my heart's content. Decorating the room would be a snap. The thing about having so much stuff is that I don't ever have to go shopping for furniture or decor. I can shop in the basement and find what I need.

Unfortunately, it took the painters an extra day to sand all the cat heads off the walls, which I felt mildly guilty about—guilty enough to let Ryan have the room when it was finished, even though it looked incredible. Ryan loved it so much I had to let him have it.

In terms of actual renovations to the Richard Harris Room, they were minimal. We needed all the available wall space for paintings, prints, and photographs. We added a long table in the middle of the room to display the ethnographic objects: masks, kapalas, and other unusual artifacts. We set up the room as we would for a traveling exhibition. We have another entire room's worth of stuff that's always on loan to various museums around the country.

The next thing I did was hire a second assistant to help us properly catalog all the pieces in the collection so that we could keep track of everything. Her duties would also include writing grants and proposals for exhibiting the items. It may sound premature to hire an assistant to handle the pieces before they arrived, but it takes a long time to put an exhibition together, and we wanted to get a jump-start on planning. We knew from experience that many places we'd dealt with in the past were booked out at least two years in advance. There was no point waiting until we had the pieces in hand to start planning how to exhibit them.

By the time Ryan left for Chicago, the Richard Harris Room was finally ready to go.

DRIVING THE COLLECTION
Ryan

The first time I went to Chicago and had dinner with Richard's family, I asked Leslie how her father was able to amass such an incredible collection. She told me that over the course of his career as an art dealer he had acquired some very valuable pieces.

"How valuable?"

"A few Rembrandts. A couple Monets."

That was incredible, but not that unusual. His access to the art world allowed him to obtain paintings that were worth quite a bit of money. I don't know how many paintings he had, but as the years went by, they became more and more valuable.

That's not the strange part. What's unusual is where he kept them: not in the bank, not in a vault, not in a temperature-controlled storage facility with around-the-clock security. He kept them under his bed. No one knew they were there.

At the time, they didn't think too much about it, Leslie explained, but in retrospect it was kind of crazy considering how valuable the paintings were. He had these priceless works of art stored under the bed with the extra blankets and missing socks. Richard had a very modest-looking home. You'd never know by looking at his house that there was a priceless art collection hidden inside. Anyone could have come in and stolen the paintings, and who knows how long it would have taken for someone to realize they were missing.

When I went to Richard's storage facility for the first time, I didn't know what to expect. I'd been warned that tracking down items from his collection could be challenging. When I told the family's middleman that I was going to the warehouse to have a look at the collection, he said two words: "Good luck."

"What do you mean?"

"You're not going to be able to see much," he said.

"How so?" I asked.

"It's very hard to find stuff in there."

"What does that mean?"

"You're going to have to tell them the number of what you're looking for, then they have to locate it, and then they can bring it."

"Okay," I said, but I didn't necessarily know what any of that meant.

I had the catalog Leslie had sent me, so I didn't anticipate any problems. How hard could it be?

That was my first mistake. Nothing could have prepared me for the size of the place. Richard's art-handling warehouse was insanely huge—I hadn't been that far off when I imagined the final scene of *Raiders of the Lost Ark*, except that nothing was out on a shelf. It was in a five-story building, and everything was secure. I couldn't go anywhere in the facility without an escort. Everything was packed away in crates and/or wrapped in plastic, so one painting looked no different from the next.

My second mistake was assuming that everything was well organized. That wasn't the case at all. The catalog I had didn't match the

HIGHLIGHTS OF THE RICHARD HARRIS COLLECTION

- *Mesoamerican Aztec vessel in the shape of a skull*
- *Seventeenth-century ceremonial cups from Nepal*
- Alegoría de la Muerte *by Tomás Mondragón*
- Death of Venus *by Roger Reutimann*

system the warehouse was using. Every time Richard put an exhibition together, he updated the catalog system for the items that were being put on display, but everything that had been left behind remained under the old, outdated system.

Let's say I was looking for a seventeenth-century painting by Adriaen van Utrecht. I couldn't say, "I'm looking for a seventeenth-century painting by Adriaen van Utrecht." I had to say, "I'm looking for P162." The art handlers would search their system for it, and half the time they wouldn't be able to find it.

It was all there, but putting my hands on a particular item was challenging. When they did find a piece I was looking for, it was either packed inside a crate or bound between two pieces of heavy-duty cardboard and wrapped in thick plastic. If I wanted to inspect a particular item, I had to crack open the crate or tear through the plastic, and then the art handlers would have to wrap it up and put it away when I was done. It was a slow, tedious process. As a result, I was only able to see about 60 percent of the items that were on my list.

My visit to Richard's art-handling warehouse was a sobering reminder of what I'd gotten myself into. I was dealing with incompatible labeling systems. I think at some point Richard was buying things and bringing them straight to the facility, where he instructed the art handlers to wrap them up and get them ready to ship because they might be in a show at some point.

It really drove home the point that Richard hardly ever got to enjoy his own collection. I'm convinced there are pieces he never saw again after he bought them. The only time he ever saw his vision come to life was at the handful of exhibitions that he did. I think those were the only moments he ever got any satisfaction out of the collection he'd spent a fortune putting together. If anything, my trip to the storage facility hardened my resolve to get Richard's work out in front of people again.

It was still worth going out there just to get a sense of how big the pieces were. This helped me figure out how I was going to get them back to Connecticut and also what we needed to do to get the house ready for them. There were a lot of moving parts, and we had very little time.

As soon as I picked up the truck at the rental place, I knew there was going to be a problem. The truck was massive: 30 feet long and 13 feet high. I'd never driven a truck that size before, and I was nervous about driving a priceless collection of art 900 miles.

I brought my friend Paul Abrahamian with me. He came along to help keep me awake and take the wheel if need be. We met Paul at the Brooklyn Oddities Flea Market some years ago. He was on the show *Big Brother* not once but twice. His claim to fame is that he was a runner-up both times he was on the show. After we met him in Brooklyn, we ran into him at LAX, and we've been friends ever since. He's an enthusiastic collector, and as Regina mentioned earlier, he films our auctions. I've become something of a mentor to him, and I try to impart a little of my knowledge about buying, selling, and restoring antiquities.

Chicago is a congested city. It has a lot of bridges and overpasses and an elevated rail system—all of which present challenges to truck drivers. On the way to the warehouse, I learned the hard way that many of those overhead obstacles are 12 feet high. I never had to think about these things while driving my car, but they presented a serious hazard to the 13-foot-tall truck I was struggling to maneuver around the city.

I had to download a GPS application that truckers use to navigate cities and towns. It was much slower than the GPS I normally use. If I missed a turn or went the wrong direction down a one-way street, which I did several times, it took forever for the map to recalibrate the route. If you've never had the pleasure of going the wrong way in a giant truck with everyone yelling and honking at you, I don't recommend it.

I hate being late. I'm never late. It's a huge pet peeve of mine. In fact, I'm notorious for being early. In spite of all the setbacks with the truck, we were on schedule until we almost reached our destination. Then, about a block away from the facility, we encountered a 12-foot overpass that would have taken the top off the truck if I hadn't been paying attention.

I had to find a different route to circumvent the overpass. The new route seemed to take us all the way around the city. This took forever, and we ended up being an hour late.

When we finally arrived at the warehouse, all of the items were down on the main floor, basically waiting for us on the loading dock, ready to be loaded into the truck. I couldn't believe how much stuff there was. All of the items were stacked on pallets and wrapped in plastic, so they looked a lot bigger. At least that's what I told myself. It looked like an enormous amount of stuff.

My first thought: *There's no way all this stuff is going to fit in the truck.* My second thought: *There's no way all this stuff is going to fit in my house.* And my third thought: *Regina is going to freak out when she sees this.*

The staff at the art warehouse were pros, and they got everything loaded into the truck in no time at all. I signed the paperwork, and we got on the road. We made it out of Chicago without any more hiccups and pointed the truck east. Paul and I stopped for gas twice but otherwise drove for fifteen hours straight. We never really stopped, and I did the bulk of the driving.

For every one of those 900 miles, I wasn't able to forget the priceless cargo that was riding behind me. There was a giant padlock on the back of the truck to keep anyone from breaking in at the gas

station, but on the road it was up to me to bring the Richard Harris
Collection home safe and sound.

• • •

UNPACKING
Regina

Ryan and Paul arrived with the truck at four in the morning and
went straight to bed. They were exhausted from driving all day
and all night, but they only slept for three or four hours before they
got up to unload the truck. Ryan seemed jittery and nervous, which
I attributed to a lack of sleep.

When he unlocked the padlock and opened up the back of the
truck, I couldn't believe my eyes. The truck was stuffed from front to
back and from floor to ceiling with crates.

"Are you kidding me?" I said.

Because Ryan went to Chicago alone, I was kept in the dark
about many of the details of the transaction. I knew we were getting
some of Richard's pieces and why, but I didn't know how many items
were coming to Connecticut. I asked Ryan, and he would tell me,
but the numbers changed every time we talked about it, so I stopped
asking. The sight of all those crates stacked in the truck told me that
might have been a mistake. I don't know what I was expecting, but
it wasn't this.

Ryan saw the look on my face and said, "It looks bigger than it is."

To demonstrate, Ryan opened up the first crate and started
removing its contents. After that, it was all a blur: paintings, pup-
pets, sculptures, and statues came flying out of the truck. There were
things in there I couldn't name. Then he tore open the next crate and
the one after that.

Titled *Death of Venus*, Roger Reutimann's statue comments on how contemporary art is thought of as an investment, which runs counter to attitudes about art centuries ago. The skull symbolizes cultural shifts, and the Ferrari-red color represents the glamour of our fast-moving modern society.

I felt so overwhelmed. Even the crates stressed me out. What were we going to do with all of them? Crates are expensive. When we shipped the Gustav Zeiller piece to Kuwait, the crate alone cost over $500. Some of the crates still had the paperwork attached from when they'd been shipped to the Wellcome Collection in London back in 2012. These were some well-traveled crates, and it made me sad to see them tossed aside once they'd served their purpose.

When Ryan unloaded Roger Reutimann's *Death of Venus*, I almost keeled over. It was so stunningly gorgeous that I didn't know what to do with myself. It's sleek, elegant, and—most importantly—modern.

As much as I love the old stuff, seeing that red skull peering out of a blood-red cowl was a thrill. Remember, I come from the world of high fashion, and seeing death presented in such a glamorous way was very exciting to me. Although stylistically it looks like it would be out of place with all our antiques, thematically it's right on point. I'm so happy to have her in our space.

That wasn't the only modern art that came off the truck: illustrations by Laurie Lipton, photography by Peruvian photographer Javier Silva-Meinel, portraits and sculptures by a Mexican-born artist from Chicago named Marcos Raya. I love contemporary Mexican art and was thrilled to see Ryan unload Raya's elaborately decorated coffin, which contained an incredibly blinged-out full-size skeleton model. If it's possible to fall in love with a work of art, that's what happened when I laid eyes on that gorgeous piece.

Surprisingly, the pieces Ryan was most excited about were the paintings, some of which were astonishingly old, like the unusual two-sided sixteenth-century *Portrait of a Man* by Barthel Bruyn the Elder, which has a figure on the front and a skull on the back. The piece that brings it all home for me is by the seventeenth-century Flemish artist Frans Francken the Younger. In *Young Death Playing the Violin*, Death serenades a wealthy old man; Death's bony foot rests on an hourglass, which is the Old World equivalent of "the clock is ticking." Death is basically saying, "Your riches don't mean a thing if you're dead." The funny thing is that the rich old man doesn't seem to care because he's still counting his money and gold trinkets while Death plays on.

The truck also contained all kinds of amazing artifacts: remnants of seventeenth-century Spanish funerary robes, a seventeenth-century Italian vanitas bust of a man in armor with a skull face, a seventeenth-century Tibetan copper Citipati panel, and a set of early nineteenth-century figurines by the German sculptor Anton Sohn depicting the Dance of Death. There seemed to be no end to the pieces coming off the truck.

It took five of us more than two days to get everything unloaded. Incredibly, there are still another fifteen or twenty pieces in Richard's warehouse that they weren't able to locate. I guess they couldn't find them in those stacks of buried treasure.

Integrating the new pieces from the Richard Harris Collection with our own collection has been a work in progress. Now that we have the pieces in our possession and have a better understanding of their astonishing beauty and cultural significance, we are working to exhibit them in a way that showcases the passion that we shared not only with Richard but with collectors everywhere. Richard accrued a collection as vast as his dreams, and we are honored to put together an exhibit that bears his name.

BEYOND *THE* WITCH'S DOOR

THE SECRET COMPARTMENT

THE CARVINGS ON THE DOOR

THE SHOW MUST GO ON

THE DOLLS HAVE THE LAST WORD

THE SECRET COMPARTMENT
Ryan

In 2023, we partnered with Atlas Obscura for a series of monthly Zoom events for members called *Antiques and Their Afterlives*. The idea was to let audiences into our home so they could spend an intimate hour with us and get a good look at some of our favorite objects. The experience opened a brief but authentic window into our lives.

One day I was preparing for a new episode while packing up some pieces for an antique show. I was working in the chapel with our assistant, Maria, and cleaning up some of the furniture, just sprucing things up for the camera. I had my eye on a cabinet we acquired from Nick that had been sitting in the corner collecting dust. At one point, I thought I'd use it in the house somewhere, but there was no longer any space. I wasn't sure what to do with the piece.

The cabinet was actually a late nineteenth-century phonograph stand. The machine sat on top of the stand, and the phonograph records were slotted into shelves on the front. A glass door, which was still intact, secured the records inside and kept the dust off them. The phonograph was invented in 1877 by Thomas Edison, and to find an early stand in such good shape was quite rare.

I can probably get $500 for this, I thought to myself. *Screw it. Let's sell it.*

We cleaned it up a little bit with some oil and polish, then wiped down the glass until it looked as good as new.

While I was inspecting our work on the back of the cabinet, I saw something I hadn't noticed before: a pair of piano hinges, which were quite small and easy to miss. Just the knuckles of the hinges were visible, and not the leaves that attach to the furniture.

"Oh, shit," I said to Maria. "I think this thing opens."

We pulled on the top of the cabinet, but it wouldn't budge.

Was it locked? If so, how?

There wasn't a keyhole or any kind of locking mechanism that we could see, but no matter what we did, we couldn't get it to open. I wondered if the top had been sealed shut with glue or stain because it clearly should open; we just couldn't figure out how.

We stumbled upon the solution by accident. We opened the glass cabinet door to inspect the top, and the secret compartment opened right up. That was the mechanism. The top of the cabinet would only open if the glass door was also open. It was so simple, but sometimes the most elegant deceptions are right in front of you.

We peered inside, and I couldn't believe what we found.

Three pistols.

Four boxes of bullets.

Two sets of handcuffs.

A pair of brass knuckles.

A police badge.

Love letters that Nick had written to his ex-wife but never sent.

After dragging the cabinet out of Nick's apartment and down three flights of stairs and then hauling it to Connecticut, where it sat in storage for almost three years, I never realized it had a secret compartment. The mystery of the missing guns had been solved—and not a moment too soon. I tried to imagine the chaos that might have unfolded if I'd sold the cabinet with the guns and ammo inside and they were discovered by some unscrupulous soul who might not be motivated to do the right thing.

I reached out to Nick's sister, and she was very happy to hear from me. We'd remained in contact over the years, and it got easier and easier to talk about Nick. She cried when I told her what we'd found. I think she was overwhelmed with emotion hearing someone outside her family talk about Nick with fondness and familiarity. We met up that weekend, and we presented her with everything that we'd found in the secret compartment. She was very touched, especially by the letters. We hadn't read them, out of respect to Nick, but it was clear they revealed yet another side of him that very few people got the opportunity to see—not even his family.

We also had another surprise for her.

Buried in Nick's papers, we'd found a black-and-white photograph of Nick's parents. The photo, from the '40s, was taken in the family's deli in Carroll Gardens. It was a moving moment for all of us—and not just because of all the delicious chicken parm that Nick had nourished us with over the years.

We don't always know what compels us to hold on to some things and let others go, but in that moment, when we were able to return the items that Nick's sister had believed were lost forever, it felt as though we'd restored a missing piece of the family's history and made it whole.

THE CARVINGS ON THE DOOR
Ryan & Regina

For as long as we've owned the Witch's Door, we've tried to find out more about it. We reached out to a few people when we first acquired it, and though no one had any insight, they gave us the names of people who might be able to help. Invariably, those people didn't have any information for us either, but they provided us with more names. Our investigation into the origins of the door continued in haphazard fashion over the next few months, and then the months turned into years.

Finally, a breakthrough of sorts. Someone had a contact at the Peabody Essex Museum in Salem, Massachusetts, and they put us in touch with the curator. This was an important contact for a reason that is fairly obvious: Salem was the epicenter of the witch hunts of the late seventeenth century.

We sent off all the information we had on the door, including photos, and a few days later the curator got back to us with good news. As near as they could tell, the door looked to be an example of first-period American architecture, which would date the door somewhere between 1625 and 1725. The curator was intrigued by both the inscriptions and the compass wheels. We hadn't paid much attention to the latter because they're much more common than the other inscriptions.

Compass wheels are circular orbs that were used to keep evil spirits away. They were essentially a deterrent and consistent with the rest of the markings on the door. Typically, these symbols were made with the use of a compass, which appears to be the case on the Witch's Door. We'd seen these orbs before and took it as a good indicator of the door's authenticity, which was why I hadn't given them much thought because the other carvings were so much more striking.

Close-up of the carved symbols on the Witch's Door

After scrutinizing the door more carefully, I found another carving that resembled the letter *W*. One could be forgiven for thinking the *W* stood for "witch"—we know we did—but that's not the case. In fact, it's not a *W* at all, but a pair of *V*s, and *VV* stands for "Virgin of Virgins," as in Mary, the mother of Jesus. The carving was a mark intended to keep demons away from the home and was used on both sides of the Atlantic. We've seen it scratched into floorboards, carved on beams, and engraved in hardware.

Although we didn't uncover anything specific about this particular door, we learned a lot. We now knew, based on the type of wood that was used for the door and the way the iron was forged, that it was native to America, as opposed to being brought to the New World from England or some other place. Also, the fact that the dealer, Roger Bacon, was an expert in witchcraft who lived relatively close to

Salem was another sign that the door hadn't strayed too far from its original home. Lastly, the carvings were all consistent with markings found on doors on or around the time of the Salem witch trials.

The next step was to determine the age of the carvings. Were they all made around the same time? I'm not an expert on antique furniture, but I've studied the carvings with a magnifying glass to see if I can detect any evidence of a mechanical tool. I didn't see anything that would indicate that the door is anything other than what it's purported to be. To my eye, the carvings look very primitive, like they were done with a knife or dagger. They're not impressive looking, which I think speaks to their authenticity.

THE SHOW MUST GO ON
Ryan & Regina

Whenever we set up the cameras for an upcoming Atlas Obscura event, I think of those fateful words a relative said during the run-up to our wedding: "Life is not a show."

Well, look at us now!

Our life is in fact one big show and probably always will be. Whether we're taking our show on the road with the Oddities Flea Market or showcasing part of our collection from our home, our business continues to evolve in new and unexpected ways. There will probably be times in our lives, like now, when our collection is expanding and times when we scale back, but it's hard to imagine letting go and selling everything.

It's like a tattoo. A lot of people don't understand tattoos. In many ways, a person's tattoos are like a *Wunderkammer*. Each tattoo marks a different time and place in our lives. We can look at any tattoo that we have on our bodies and remember the circumstances in which we got it.

Are all of them masterpieces? No, some of them aren't all that great, to be honest, but even the best tattoo will fade over time, becoming more imperfect every day. That doesn't mean we love them any less. When we look at each tattoo, we remember the story of how it came to be, where we were, and what we were doing. Even if the tattoo itself doesn't mean anything—sometimes a tattoo is just a tattoo—the story associated with getting it is meaningful and calls to mind very specific feelings.

A collection of tattoos is like a cabinet of curiosities in which each object was collected at a different time in your life, and each tells its own story. But taken together, they tell a larger story about you.

What's the next chapter of our story?

We have no idea. When we began this book in 2023, we didn't know that we would be partnering with the Richard Harris estate to exhibit his collection. That experience alone has taught us so much about what's important to us, why we do what we do, and where we should go from here.

When we die, no one's going to want our collection. There isn't an institution or establishment out there that's waiting to take it and put it on view. And we don't have kids to pass it on to: "It's all yours! Now go do something with it." We don't know what the future looks like for us, but we talk about it all the time. *What's going to happen to all of our stuff?*

Richard tried so hard to donate his collection to a museum, but no one could facilitate it. It must have been heartbreaking for him to spend his life building this beautiful collection and realizing that, at the end of the day, while the individual pieces had value, the collection as a whole did not. So he did what he never wanted to do: He sold it off.

Richard's children and, presumably, grandchildren will benefit from the sale. As we don't have children, we're going to have to sell our collection before we get old and frail. It will go one of three ways: One day we'll wake up and decide to sell everything—the house, the collection, every last thing. Then we'll move far away and either start all over again or open up an antique store in some bucolic town.

Quis evadet (Who will be spared?). Bone, wood, polychrome, and brass by Ryan Matthew Cohn.

Or we'll keep trading up, selling several lesser items to buy one excellent piece. Then, instead of a thousand pieces, we would have ten. That would make Regina happy.

A possible third path is for Ryan to keeping making art, but instead of combining collections, we merge individual pieces together to create radical assemblages that are part anatomical preparation and part antique art. At least that way our name will be attached to the art forever.

We don't know. That's why it was so important for us to write this book. To tell the stories of the fascinating people we've met on this long, strange road we've traveled. To tell the story of the professor's widow, Max Wax, Nick Parmesan, Richard Harris, and all the others. They traveled to incredible places and collected amazing artifacts from around the world, and instead of seeing their name on an old auction catalog, you can read their stories in this book.

When we invite people over to our home to look at our collection, the tour seldom lasts more than a few minutes. Then we sit down together and tell stories about where all these objects came from and the odd and unusual people who brought them into our lives. The Old Masters were right: You can't take it with you, but as long as we draw breath, we can share stories about the places we went, the things we saw, and the strange and wonderful people who enriched our lives along the way.

THE DOLLS HAVE THE LAST WORD
Ryan & Regina

We thought we were done with this book. The manuscript was literally on its way to the copy editor when some very unusual things happened.

It started when we asked our friend David Zeck to come over to our house and photograph some of the objects, including the Charlie McCarthy dolls. We moved the dolls downstairs to where we were having the shoot and left them sitting on a chair. During the course of the shoot, we said some rude things about the dolls. We don't want to repeat what was said, but when David asked us, "Aren't you the least bit superstitious?" we replied, "Why would we be? They're just objects!"

Apparently, the dolls didn't care for that.

After the shoot, we put them back on the shelf in the library. We were only gone a few minutes when we heard a loud crash. We came back and found them sprawled on the floor with their mouths hanging open. The dolls' mouths are attached to a metal bar with a length of string that holds their little mandibles in place. Somehow, the strings had become detached. This had never happened before. It's almost as if the strings had snapped!

We put them back on the shelf, and this time we anchored them in place so we could work in peace. A couple of hours went by, and the same thing happened again. The dolls came crashing down to the floor. When we went back to the library, one of the dolls had cracked its head during the fall. Both mouths were hanging open again, as if they were trying to tell us something.

The vibe around the house became very tense. Strange and unsavory circumstances started to occur. The heater in our guesthouse suddenly stopped worked. Packages got lost in the mail or were sent to the wrong address. While we were in the city, our car disappeared, only to reappear the next day a few blocks away. The Globe Theatre, where we hold our events in LA, informed us they were shutting down for good.

Were these just strange coincidences, or were there other forces in play? We are very meticulous when it comes to the details, and even if our string of bad luck was due to feeling distracted and over-whelmed, why were we feeling these things so intensely? We *always* have a million things going on.

This was different. It got to the point where we were afraid to go into the library at night.

We reached out to a friend named Beckie-Ann Galentine who has experience with the paranormal. She told us that what we were experiencing was very common, especially with dolls, and that they were acting out by causing chaos. She advised us to do what many people had been suggesting to us since the earlier incidents with the dolls: talk to them and make amends.

We went up to the library and sat with the dolls. We apologized for disrespecting them and promised to do our best to make sure they were comfortable and always felt welcome in our home. We also mended the cracks and fixed the jaws that had become detached.

After that, all the weirdness came to an abrupt end. The bad luck stopped and in some cases turned around. The heating repair turned out to be minor. The packages that had been lost were found. At three in the morning the night after we apologized to the dolls, we got an email from the Globe Theatre in LA, telling us they were back in business and had signed a fourteen-year lease. This was after *LA Weekly* had published an article declaring the Globe had shut its doors for good.

We don't know what to make of this. When you experience something like this, you feel like you know less than when you started out. There's no clarity, no grand explanation like in the movies. We've made our peace with the dolls, but whether they've made their peace with us remains to be seen.

CABINET OF CURIOSITIES EXPLAINED

1. Tibetan kapala skull.—2. Turned and carved cup made from a gourd, red coral, and bone.—3. Sterling silver filigree vessel used to hold a seventeenth-century bezoar.—4. Eighteenth-century reliquary from Italy containing the fragments of a saint.—5. Nineteenth-century *Gorgonocephalus eucnemis* (basket starfish) on a stand.—6. Eighteenth-century Spanish santos bust made out of wood and polychrome.—7. Bronze "Death" figure that once belonged to famed jewelry designer Kenneth Jay Lane.—8. Early primitive water vessel.—9. Carved Japanese boxwood Netsuke of a skull.—10. Eighteenth-century Spanish wood and polychrome santos figure.—11. Eighteenth-century turned wood hourglass.—12. Chinese puzzle ball made of jade.—13. Nineteenth-century medical preparation showing how teeth sit in the maxilla and mandible.—14. Victorian taxidermied domestic kitten.—15. Eighteenth-century carved ivory figure.—16. Nineteenth-century posed hand made of wax.—17. Japanese ivory Okimono of a skull adorned with a snake.—18. Victorian articulated fish skull.—19. Nineteenth-century copper enameled Tibetan skull.—20. Hornbill bird skull.—21. Pair of eighteenth-century feet belonging to a Spanish cage doll.—22. Pre-Colombian Aztec vessel circa 1300–1519 AD.—23. Seventeenth-century turned wood chalice with bone lid topper.—24. Antique red coral cluster.—25. Seventeenth-century ceremonial cup from Nepal made from a nautilus shell.—26. Victorian taxidermy bird diorama.—27. Eighteenth-century Italian bronze candlestick adorned with winged cherubs—28. Victorian taxidermy turtle with hand-painted Italian crabapple.

BIBLIOGRAPHY

Castner, James L. *Shrunken Heads: Tsantsa Trophies and Human Exotica*. Feline Press, 2002.

Ebenstein, Joanna, ed. *Death: A Graveside Companion*. Thames and Hudson, 2017.

Fitzharris, Lindsey. *The Butchering Art: Joseph Lister's Quest to Transform the Grisly World of Victorian Medicine*. Farrar, Straus and Giroux, 2017.

Gambino, Paul. *Morbid Curiosities: Collections of the Macabre and the Bizarre.* Laurence King, 2016.

Mauriès, Patrick. *Cabinets of Curiosities*. Thames and Hudson, 2019.

Weschler, Lawrence. *Mr. Wilson's Cabinet of Wonder: Pronged Ants, Horned Humans, Mice on Toast, and Other Marvels of Jurassic Technology*. Vintage Books, 1996

PHOTOGRAPHY
CREDITS

Photography credits by page number:

Pages ii, xii, 6, 17, 28, 32, 41, 48, 55, 79, 102, 130, 134, 135, 142, 154, 159, 162, 172, 178, 198, 203, 206, 230, 237, 241, 255, 265, 268: David Zeck

Pages 8, 10, 30, 37, 50, 60, 68, 74, 76, 88, 93, 104, 107, 110, 115, 121, 127, 132, 156, 165, 168, 175, 185, 188, 193, 208, 210, 223, 258: courtesy of Ryan Cohn and Regina Rossi

Page 83: Danny Goldshtein

Pages 87, 91, 97, 98: David Bowles

Page 125: Steve Prue

Page 139: Jesse Korman

Page 180: Maria Cromm

Page 217: Katrin Albert

Page 228: Roger Reutimann

Page 272: Nicolas Bruno

Photography credits for photographic insert:

Pages 1, 2, 4–7: David Zeck

Page 3: Ryan Cohn

Page 8: Roger Reutimann

ACKNOWLEDGMENTS

We have learned that all books are collaborations, and we feel the same way about our careers. Without the guidance, enthusiasm, and support of countless people, we wouldn't be where we are today. Here's a partial list of people who mean the world to us.

Ryan thanks: The Cohn family, especially my mother and father for nurturing and encouraging all of my artistic endeavors, and my siblings Evan, Shaun, and Jennifer, and nephews and nieces Anthony, Gabby, Sophie, and Elijah. I'm also indebted to my mentor, Arnold Goldstein.

Regina thanks: My mom and dad, Robert and Norma Rossi. My only wish is that you were able to see my success. Matthew Rossi and Samira, thank you for my beloved niece, Ainara: I hope you always love Halloween and stay curious and full of wonder. Uncle Nicky, Claudia, and Doug Plyler. In loving memory of Auntie Theresa. And to Betsey Johnson, I'm proud to be a "pink lady" for life.

We both thank: Leslie Harris, Mark Harris, Barbara Harris, Tom Lamb, and the rest of the Harris family for entrusting us with Richard's beautiful and legendary collection. Nick Martino, Maria Cromm, and all of the Martino family. Tim and Karrie League from Alamo Drafthouse Cinema, House of Wax Bar, Billy Leroy, "Auntie" Joni Van Stavern, "Honest" David Zeck, Christophe "Frenchy" Bardot, Jake Mueser and Amber Doyle, Robert Anthony DeFalco,

Karen Wellikoff, David L. Bowles and the cast and crew of the show *Oddities*, Andy Animal, Josh Styles, Danny Goldshtein and the Stalkers family, Maria Valdovinos-Arceo, Nicolas Bruno, Kat Lemcke, Jenny Smith, Melissa Matteo, Christina Lu, and Leah Snow.

Our beloved pets, both past and present: Ozzy, Percy Blue, Princess Andromeda, Wolfie, Spider-Baby, Birdie, Herman, and Regina's childhood pet bird, Spirit.

Thank you to all the talented people who helped make this book possible, but especially Liz Vap for spearheading the project, Peter McGuigan for his vision, and Lynn Grady for taking a chance on us. Thank you to Gabrielle White and Madeline Shellhouse at Ultra Literary; Pamela Geismar, Michelle Triant, Jessica Tackett, Cecilia Santini, Rachael Marks, and Kim Dayman at Chronicle Books; and Judith Riotto. We would also like to thank the incredibly talented Jim Ruland for helping us get our thoughts onto paper during the process of writing this book. We are proud to have you as an honorary member of our odd family. We truly appreciate all of your hard work and passion. Thank you for giving us a chance to tell our stories!

Lastly, we thank all of our friends, vendors, patrons, and followers who have supported the Oddities Flea Market over the years and have contributed to our odd community.

ABOUT THE AUTHORS

RYAN MATTHEW COHN is an artist, curator, art collector, and cofounder of the Oddities Flea Market. His artwork has been exhibited at the Museum of Arts and Design, Armour-Stiner Octagon House, Copro Gallery, Last Rites Gallery, Morbid Anatomy Museum, Roq La Rue Gallery, and more. His curatorial work has appeared in *Playboy, Revolver,* and *The New York Times*, and in the films such as *Wonderstruck* and *The Greatest Showman*. Between 2010 and 2014, Ryan was featured as one of the stars on the Discovery Channel show *Oddities*, and he currently appears on the web series *Antiques and Their Afterlives* on Atlas Obscura. Ryan is a highly sought-after collector who specializes in rare and unusual antiques and artifacts related to science, anatomy, natural history, and memento mori.

REGINA M. ROSSI is the cofounder and producer of the Oddities Flea Market, a traveling high-end art market. Under her leadership, the Oddities Flea Market expanded from Brooklyn to Los Angeles, Chicago, Seattle, Manhattan, and beyond. In 2016, she collaborated with her husband, Ryan, to curate Brooklyn's House of Wax, a bar, museum, and event space like no other. With a background in high-end fashion, Regina brings glamour and elegance to her exhibits and events.

Ryan and Regina live in Connecticut with their cat, three dogs, and growing collection of rare art, oddities, and other ephemera. *The Witch's Door* is their first book.